ACKNOWL

MW00932574

I want to thank my Lord and Savior Jesus Christ for seeing it fit to trust me with this assignment. There were times I did not understand my journey or purpose but because of my grandmother, Essie Pearl Rogers, prayers and her introducing me to God's word at an early age, my faith remained solid and I've been able to walk into God's calling for my life.

When I first began writing *"...And What If You Live?,"* I had no intention for volume 1 to focus on my divine appointments. My journey exemplifies the impact one can make on the lives of others by allowing God to appoint us for His good. While some are mentioned, please know that I've had numerous divine appointments along my journey who have blessed me in countless ways and I am forever grateful. I humbly recognize that without these appointed angels there would not be an *"...And What If You Live?: Divine Appointments, Volume 1."*

Last, to the Board of Directors for *"...And What If You Live?"* I asked you to believe in my vision and say yes to the unknown and you graciously accepted the challenge. I am thankful for your "yes" and I appreciate your sacrifices to fulfill our mission of assisting those seeking to move forward from a diagnosis and life change to discover new direction, create new purpose, and live more aligned with their values. I could not have asked for a more committed group of individuals to lead. *....And What If You Live?*

DEDICATION

*For their sacrifice, love and faith I proudly dedicate this
book in memory of my parents,*

Adell and Charlie Ray Stevens Jr.

*Mom and Dad, your legacy will continue to live through
me. I pray I can birth the dreams you didn't have a chance to
live.*

May you continue to rest in perfect peace.

Your daughter forever,

Janeen

CONTENTS

FOREWORD

My thoughts on the woman who wrote this book? She's kind, brilliant, resilient, loving, and she is so caring of others. Ray Janeen Stevens has to be one of the sweetest women I know.

Rarely do you hear stories about meeting people who have been appointed to you for your life journey in a hospital bed fighting for their life, but that is how I met my mom. After meeting her, there was such a strong connection that to this day is difficult to explain to others. Meeting someone for the first time and knowing that you never want to lose contact is almost unheard of however, this is what I felt when I met Ray Janeen Stevens.

This connection is one that I could never have imagined or thought was possible for my life. She's someone I never knew I needed. Seven years ago, she became my mother at heart and I love her dearly.

I was working in housekeeping at Cooper Hospital in Camden, NJ and I remembered seeing her laying in the hospital bed. She had so many tubes connected to her. I didn't have a clue what she could've possibly have been through but I do know that from that moment my life had changed and so did hers. It amazes me how God works in us. I undeniably know that seeing her that day was meant to be. It was a gift from God.

Clocking into work that particular day was divine timing. I was at the lowest point of my life and cannot put into words what my thoughts were. I somehow made it into work knowing I didn't have the courage or strength to make it through the day. Today I know the strength I had was from God.

As I entered her hospital room, I was trying to be as quiet as possible and I remember feeling so many emotions that day. I entered the room to begin sweeping, but I wanted to silently cry. I couldn't see myself that day but somehow, she saw me. She said to me,

"Honey, I don't know what it is that you are going through but God told me to tell you everything is going to be okay."

I thought, how is this possible? Her back was to me and after many hours of surgery she saw me. How could she see me?"

I had reached a low point in my life and I was seeking God and, in that moment, He used Ray Janeen to speak to me. I knew she was an angel that was sent specifically for me. I could not comprehend exactly what I felt at the time but I knew this was someone I wanted in my life forever and I knew she was a divine appointment. She was mine and I was hers. This was God's plan.

Throughout the book she speaks on her amazing journey and how God uses her as she forms divine connections through this thing, we call life. With all that has happened throughout her diagnosis and loss, she talks about the start of her nonprofit *"...And What If You Live?"* as it will encourage you to trust God and know that you're not alone. Her journey encourages others to go to Him when you seek answers.

As I think today on how she made it through her storm I know it will encourage others. She explains the importance of communicating the things you are going through because although it may feel like the end you also have to consider…and what if you live?

To my mom, Ray Janeen Stevens, I love you so much. I am so proud of you and all that you do to help others and fulfill the purpose God has placed on your life.

…And What If You Live?

-Jameka Tahira Fisher

INTRODUCTION

My Challenges Do Not Define Me

Triple Negative Breast Cancer, BRCA 2 Gene, 5 Surgeries in 8 Months, Self Lovenox Injections to Prevent Blood Clots, Ten Rounds of Chemotherapy , DIEP Flap Surgery, Left Breast Fine Needle Biopsy, Lymph Node Dissection, Bilateral Mastectomy, 2 Breast Revisions, Hysterectomy for Ovarian and Pancreatic Cancer Prevention, Tooth Extractions from Chemotherapy, Enlarged Thyroid; Biopsy, Thyroid Lobectomy, Joint Pain, Memory Loss, Hair Loss, Change In Eyesight, Weight Gain, Hernia, Exhaustion, Muscle Atrophy, Shortness of Breath, Colonoscopy, Survivors Guilt, Trauma, PTSD, Child Barren, (Being Adopted Always Wanted Children That Looked Like Me), Numerous Doctor Appointments to Schedule, Oncology Appointments For The Rest of My Life, Pet Scans, X-Rays, MRI & CT Scans, Caregiving While Needing a Caregiver, Anxiety of Recurrence (forever) But God.

None of this defines me. I am not only a survivor but a thriver ...*And What If You Live?*

Have you ever wanted to give up? For me it was an aggressive breast cancer diagnosis but for you it may be something completely different that halted you in your tracks and took away your desire to keep moving forward.

This book was written to provide help, enlightenment, support and encouragement for days you feel like giving up. I want you to know that you are seen and are important to God. It is my intent for this book to give you light and hope in darkness.

Through my diagnosis, life disappointments and challenges I've found that God is the same God and is in control of our lives. He will put divine appointments in place to help us throughout our course of life, however we must activate our faith and trust Him.

I make a conscious decision every day to not only survive but thrive so I can help others to do the same. God gave me a will to live and I want the same for you.

Thank you for taking this journey with me.

"I was so excited to read Divine Appointments by Ray Janeen Stevens because it's in those connections we find the strength to leap and ask the question, "...And what if you live?" This book is a journey unfolded, and a miracle lived!'

- Coach Dena Billups
  Founder of ART of Training and Development, LLC

Chapter 1
Born Bobbie Jo Mitchell

"For my father and my mother have forsaken me, but the Lord will take me in." [1]

---

[1] *Psalms 27:10 ESV*

May 10th, 1990 was the day I was told my birth name and the first time I saw someone who looked like me. This was the day I met my biological mother, Cathy Jo. This was a day I will never forget and a day that changed my life forever.

I've always known that I was adopted. At an early age I was always a curious child and would ask my parents questions like,

"Why is the sky blue or why do I need to play outside when grown-ups are talking?"

This particular day I asked my mom,

"Where do babies come from?"

The answer I received from my mother was one I did not expect. I remember her getting my brother and my dad, sitting us down and telling me that I was their daughter but instead of coming out of her belly I had arrived in a car. To say I was confused is an understatement. I think I asked,

"What kind of car?"

Again, I always had a question. All I knew was that I was loved, had a beautiful home, delicious meals, toys galore and that I was "home." I knew as a child what safety felt like and I was thankful.

As I got older, I would sometimes wonder about my biological mother. I was told she was 14 when she gave birth to me and as a teenager, I could only imagine how hard the decision would be to carry a baby as a child and give that baby away. As I look back, as a teen I think I was so scared of getting pregnant because I never wanted to be put in the position of not being able to take care of my baby or to give him or her to the care of someone else.

When I was a sophomore in high school, I became very sick and almost died. I remember having these horrible, debilitating headaches that would stay for days. One day I was in the cafeteria at school and told a friend about the sharp pains I was having on my right temple. I felt tremendous pain and as if I was going to pass out. My mother was called and took me to the emergency room. They told her that I had a severe case of viral meningitis and that if I were not treated, I could have died. I was so ill that I could not finish the school year and no one could tell me how I caught this and became so sick. The doctor told my mom that there were genetic factors that lead to people developing meningitis. It was during this time that I knew there were questions I needed answered about my health, things that I needed to know. Yes, I was still that girl with questions.

The early part of May 1990 I remember watching the talk show Donahue with my mother. On that show he was interviewing adoptees and an organization called The Adoptees Liberty Movement, ALMA. I heard the emotional stories of how people met their biological parents. My mother and I discussed calling the number to see if my biological mother signed up for this registry and if she was looking for me.

On May 10th, 1990, I remember going to work at the Weathervane in a local mall. I had this number to ALMA that I had been carrying with me in my wallet. I remember asking the store manager to go into her office to make a "quick" call. I briefly told her about the show and what I wanted to do just to know but I was not expecting anything to come from it.

When I called the number, someone answered after 2 rings; I was going to hang up after the third ring. The woman on the other end sounded so pleasant and asked three questions. My birth surname, the hospital I was born in and the year I was born. I answered all three questions and she asked me the number I was calling her from and then she asked me to hold on the line. She must have been gone for maybe two minutes but it seemed like hours. When she came back on the line she was crying and told me that she had great news.

My biological grandmother joined the registry 6 years prior and had been searching for me. I almost passed out. She asked if she could call my grandmother and to give her my number at the store. I told her,

"Yes."

A short time later the phone rang, it was my grandmother. She said,

"Hello Janeen, I'm your grandmother and I love you."

I then heard screams and cheers in the background. I would later find out they were her co-workers. She told me that she lived in a neighboring town twenty miles away and wanted to come see me before leaving town the next day. I called my parents who told me,

"Tell her to come."

That night not only did she come but also my biological mother, her husband and three of my siblings. There was no doubt I was related to them. When my grandmother arrived, she told my mother,

"Thank you for taking care of my granddaughter."

My mother put her hand over her heart and said,

"I took care of my daughter."

Those words spoken by my mother would define our relationship for years to come.

When I looked at my biological mother for the first time it was like looking in the mirror. We talked the same, our mannerisms were similar and through her eyes I saw pain we were both functioning through that would not be talked about for years to come. Meeting my biological mother and family afforded me the opportunity to learn and grow; it is something I will never regret. As I'm still learning and understanding our relationship, I realize there is so much to share about us that will heal a multitude.

That night my biological mother told me she hid me for six months out of fear she would be forced to abort me. She explained that she did not know how I survived the intense labor because of the medication she was on. My mother told her I had jaundice and issues with my right leg when I was brought to her home at three days old as their foster child. I remember knowing in that moment that God had His hands on me, my life and journey.

My biological mother told me she named me Bobbie Jo from a tv series called Petticoat Junction. Cathy naming me before giving me up for adoption meant so much to me. The fact that my parents, Adell and Charlie Ray made me my father's namesake gave me a sense of belonging, acceptance, security and legacy. I am Ray Janeen Stevens.

Over the time Cathy and I spent developing our relationship I learned so much about strength and perseverance. To be honest I needed her for this during certain seasons of my life. She was beautiful, truly she was! I remember looking at her in awe of her beauty. When looking at her you would never know the health battles she faced. To my knowledge and as per our conversations Cathy had multiple sclerosis and sarcoidosis. Her ability to manage her illnesses and maintain her daily life was admirable.

A divine appointment is defined as a meeting which was inspired and led by God. Outside of my parents, Cathy was one of my first divine appointments. In that instance I knew our meeting was set up by God for such a time as this. I believe our introduction was designed to help us both during a time we needed peace, understanding, acceptance and healing. I was able to let her know that I never carried any animosity or anger knowing I was given up for adoption but instead a grateful heart knowing she loved me enough to give me a life she could not as a 14-year-old mother.

I know our meeting gave her peace from a letter I received from her 13 days after our initial meeting. The letter is dated May 23rd, 1990, and reads:

Dear Janeen, just wanted you to know that I was thinking wonderful thoughts of you. You're everything I hoped you would be plus more. Every time the phone rings, I hope that it's you. I'm so very proud of you. I'm so very proud to have a daughter as precious as you. You have set such a fine example for Evan, Travis and yes, even little Kaysie and whenever your name is mentioned, their eyes light up.

Because I expressed my love for you to Rodney all of the sixteen years that we've been together, he loves you too. He says, it's as if you were always there. We always thought about you and wondered if you were alive, if you were cared for, if you were hurting. You've always been with us. He knew that you were a part of me and that if he wanted me, he knew that he needed to accept you too, even if I didn't have you. He knew you would always be in my thoughts, in my heart and in my soul.

Always remember that I'm here for you. I can't turn back the hands of time, but I can take each moment of my life now and love you and help you as a young woman.

You are so beautiful inside and out. God has truly blessed me. He has made me so happy.

I pray and hope for your happiness and success as your life continues. Other people may focus on "material" success, but I pray for your "inner" success, as a woman. Your self-worth, not in any human's eyes, but in God's eyes. I love you now and always.

Love forever,

Mommy

As our relationship grew, it was not perfect but it was ours. One thing I learned throughout our journey was that it's important to love without expectation. I believe we at times had expectations without understanding we were individuals with life experiences before reuniting as adults. We were only 14 years apart and this walk was new to both of us. There were sides of her she did not share, her vulnerability, fear of rejection and life she dreamed of that was deferred by unexpected life events, one being me. As I look back, Cathy did not have a say or choice as to how I left or re-entered her life. I've learned that being open to seeing the people we love in their totality enables us the opportunity for acceptance and forgiveness. We don't know the cost of others nor do they know our cost.

God loved me enough to remove the question of who my biological mother was and if she loved me. No matter how our relationship changed over the years to follow, I truly believe she loved me but with the guarded heart of a 14-year-old girl who had her newborn baby taken from her without consent.

I've been told that making the call on May 10th, 1990 was brave but to me it was radical faith, the faith God put in me as a little girl confirming that all things are possible to those who believe. My faith rested in God's promises and His word. He would give me the desires of my heart. Unbeknownst to me my heart needed to know Cathy and her journey. I would later find that radical faith comes with a cost.

Chapter 2
Radical Faith

"For you know that the testing of your faith produces

steadfastness." [2]

In 2002, I was working in the marketing department for a utility in Philadelphia. One day I came home from work and while going through the mail I came across an appeal letter from a local non-profit asking for monetary support to assist teens aging out of foster care. I immediately thought of my life and the blessings of having my foster parents who thankfully adopted me; became my parents and gave me a family and loving home.

At that moment I knew I wanted to make a difference in the lives of others, and within a week enrolled in a master's program in nonprofit management at Eastern University. Within three months I applied for a Development Director position at Children's Aid Society in Norristown, Pa. I remember walking into the first interview to meet the phenomenal Peter Cogan who had been Executive Director for the organization for almost 30 years. I had no experience except my desire to help others whose stories could have been mine.

My meeting with Peter went amazingly well and he asked me to come back for a second interview. I felt so confident that day and I was so eager to come back in hopes of getting an offer to accept the position. When I arrived for the interview, the administrative assistant told me they were ready for me. I remember thinking, *"they?"*

When I entered the room, I saw fifteen board members looking at me with questions for me to answer. I froze. It was one of the most embarrassing, humiliating experiences of my life. I remember going home to my apartment bursting into tears asking God,

"Why would you bring this opportunity to me to have it taken?"

I knew my moment had passed but I would learn God has the final say. I sent the best thank you letter I could to Mr. Cogan and the Board of Directors in hope that they would find it in their hearts to see beyond my nervousness and moments of imposter syndrome.

A week later I received a call that Mr. Cogan wanted to meet with me. I thought it was kind of him to meet with me in person to say it wasn't my time and he did not see me as qualified for the position. Instead, he told me that he saw me and even though that interview was not my best, and after interviewing over 10 candidates, he and the board of directors wanted me for the position. He was sure that I was the right person to lead the development office. That day I became one of the first African American female Development Directors in Southeastern Pennsylvania.

Divine appointment is where your fear meets favor. Jesus reaches out His hand through our fear to rescue us. Be assured that God is present in your fear and inadequacies. He can give you favor in the midst of what others deem impossible.

This opportunity changed my career path and gave me new aspirations and purpose. For years to come God would enable me to manage and direct the development offices for various nonprofit organizations. God had plans for me.

"For I know the plans I have for you, declares the Lord, plans to prosper you and not harm you, plans to give you a hope and a future." [3]

In 2012, I began working at a nonprofit organization in Philadelphia. I remember there were many days of traveling into the city at 8am and leaving at 9:30 or 10:00 pm. Upon taking this position I had just ended a relationship with someone I thought would be my husband. God, I thank you for divine appointments and intervention. Instead of taking time to grieve the relationship I became engrossed in my new role.

In January 2013 I remember clearly hearing God say,

"It's time to buy your house."

On that very day I made a call to get pre-approved for a mortgage and committed to the process of buying my first home.

I purchased my home and surprised my mother by telling her I had a first-floor bedroom and bath just for her. I closed on my home May 16th of 2013. May 16th is my parents' wedding anniversary and I was able to fulfill a promise I made to my father, prior to his passing of taking care of my mother.

It may seem odd to many but within a month after purchasing my home I understood clearly that God was calling me to resign from my job. I want to reiterate that I had just purchased my home, used a lot of my savings for the down

---

[3] *Jeremiah 29:11 ESV*

payment and renovations, had my elderly mother with me and I felt called to walk away from my job. I had roughly 4 months' worth of savings to sustain our household until God revealed what He had for me next. I walked away with nothing but the promise of unemployment compensation.

"Now faith is the assurance of things hoped for, the conviction of things not seen." [4]

I had radical faith and was certain on obeying and trusting God's instructions. I went through the process of applying for jobs close to home and did not get called for interviews. This had never happened to me and I could not understand why it was happening now. I did what I felt God wanted me to do, so why am I not being called back from the nonprofit organizations I was applying to?

I asked God to give me anything to sustain me during this time of transition. I then was offered and accepted a position at a local mortgage company. This was humbling as my salary was far less than what I was used to but for the first time in years, even with the change in salary I was not "on" 24/7; I had time to be still.

After being with this company for five months, my supervisor was interviewing for a fortune 500 company and mentioned that it would be a great opportunity for me. He mentioned the salary and potential for growth. When I heard the

---

[4] *Hebrews 11:1 ESV*

name of the company my first thoughts were that this would be a great opportunity to get in the door to work for their foundation.

I interviewed for this company and a non-profit organization in Camden, NJ the same week and received job offers from both. I felt that accepting the offer for the non-profit organization would best fit my skill set but there was an overwhelming calling to accept the offer from the fortune 500 company and so I did. Radical faith is thanking God even before we see his promises. I now understand the importance of obedience. I had no idea that God was preparing me for a storm that was coming.

Chapter 3
Through the Storm

"And he awoke and rebuked the wind and said to the sea, "Peace! Be still!" And the wind ceased, and there was a great calm." [5]

---

[5] *Mark 4:39*

April 20th, 2015 was the day I started my new position. It was less stressful, close to home, had amazing potential and benefits. Everything seemed to be going perfect - I could finally live more comfortably financially and not count every dime and I believed this is where God wanted me to be in this season.

On June 20th, 2015, I woke up to a call from my cousin Tuwanda. We would generally touch base on Saturday mornings to catch up from the week. I remember being excited to tell her about a date I had the night prior. Being a caregiver to my mother did not afford me the opportunity to get out often. My mother did not like to be home alone during the night and truth be told, I did not feel comfortable leaving her alone.

As I began to tell my animated story she made a comment that made me laugh. I touched my right breast and felt a lump. It was so pronounced that I immediately told her I needed to call her back. When I went in the bathroom, I looked at my breast and did not see any bruising or discoloration; however, upon touch it was solid, hard and the size of a quarter. I knew something was wrong. I continued to pose in the mirror hoping that if I moved my arm a certain way the lump would disappear but it did not. I stayed upstairs in my room for over an hour googling different sites to get a better understanding of what this may be because I refused to believe it was cancer. I was healthy, never heard of anyone in my biological family having this concern, and God would not do this to me. I was not perfect but I was living my life to glorify him. I gave my life to

Christ, accepted Him as my personal savior, honored my parents, cared for my elderly mother, so there is no way he would let this happen to me.

I immediately knew this was a test of my faith and I needed to just wait until my appointment to confirm the mass was benign and I did not have breast cancer. I never told anyone other than my cousin about the significance of the lump. I continued as if nothing was happening inside my body. My mother did not have a clue as I did not want her to know and worry about me. This would be too much for her to handle. We had a date at Perkins and Boscov's, also a visit to my father's gravesite. The next day was Father's Day and in a strange way I felt like my dad was trying to tell me something and finding this lump was a message from him. My faith was radical and, in this moment, I did not fear the storm because in my mind it was calm. I had no idea of the storm that was coming.

I had just had my mammogram six months prior. The technician mentioned a small spot, but also believed it could've been a shadow and would send the findings for further review. A few weeks later I got a postcard in the mail stating that I was fine and there were no abnormalities in my mammogram. Knowing this made me feel even more confident that I would be cleared from a cancer diagnosis.

On Monday when scheduling an appointment with gynecology, I realized that I did not have health insurance until July 21st and it was only June 22nd. And with a new diagnosis it would be difficult for me to get life insurance. My anxiety went into overdrive. I said to myself,

"How much is this appointment going to cost me?"

"What if there are no more appointments before July 21st?"

"What if my employer finds out and lets me go?"

My head was spinning. In 2013 after leaving the non-profit organization I had signed up for Obama Care. I made a phone call to healthcare.gov and was told my insurance was active until July 31st. I had time to make appointments and be seen by a doctor, however I had no approved time off from work. I was under a 90-day probationary period as a new employee and could not get time off from work until July 21st. I felt the pressure.

I was able to schedule an appointment to see a gynecologist at Cooper Hospital in Camden, NJ. My previous mammogram was also done at Cooper Hospital so the doctor had complete access to my medical history. After the appointment, the doctor told me that she thought it could simply be a benign cyst or mass because I was overall healthy and had no history of cancer in my biological family. She referred me to a radiologist for further testing.

On the ride home I felt as if I was about to encounter a storm that was going to test my faith and everything I knew God promised me through His word. I was almost home and got a call from my mother telling me to hurry home because the newscaster said a storm was on the way. I managed to make it home just in time. I looked out my bedroom window and saw rain pour like I hadn't seen in years. I could not see the street outside my house until 15 minutes later, the rain had stopped and the sky was a beautiful orange and blue with clouds passing through. Then in the distance I saw a rainbow. I believe this was God telling me to hold on and know that He is still God.

A week later I had an appointment with radiology. I was able to extend my lunch break without pay for this doctor's visit. I believe I told my employer it was for a previously scheduled appointment prior to my start date that could not be changed. The radiologist was so kind, comforting and thorough. The test was painful due to the pressure used to get an accurate reading during the test. She acknowledged the mass was prominent but was hopeful it was not cancer. She said I would get a call within a week to advise me of her findings.

While at work, on Friday July 17th, 2015, at 12:15pm I received a call from the radiologist. I quickly took the call and went outside to speak with her. Her tone did not sound the same as it did when I saw her last. She began to tell me that she had my test results and wanted to refer me to a well-respected breast surgeon based on the extensive growth of the mass. I asked her if it was cancer and did not hear the confidence in her voice as she began to tell me the words I did not expect to hear. All I heard was,

"I wish I did not have to give you this news but the mass you found is indeed cancer."

I asked her what stage and she advised me that the breast surgeon would give me that information. I begged her to tell me and she told me that based on what she saw it looked to be stage 3. I asked her,

"Well, how many stages are there?"

She said,

"4."

I remember thinking that this was not my life and this could not be true. How and why is this happening? I immediately went back inside and began to finish my workday as if nothing had happened. I did not want anyone to know due to fear of losing my new job and health benefits that I would now need more than ever.

I constantly looked at the clock waiting for my shift to end because I had so many emotions that could not be seen or expressed. The irony of waiting for time to speed up when really all I wanted was more time, more time to live. At the end of my workday, I went to my car, and drove towards home. I screamed, yelled and let out a cry that scared me. This was happening too fast and I did not have a moment to process what was happening to my mind, body and faith.

On my way home I called two close friends to help me make sense of what was happening. Although they meant well, I felt alone in this journey and I had questions. I did not know of anyone else that had a breast cancer diagnosis and to my knowledge no one in my biological family had been diagnosed, so how did I get this and at such an advanced stage?

I parked my car near home and called my biological mother in hopes of getting a better understanding of family medical history as it related to cancer. I called her and did not get an answer. I left a voicemail for her to call me back and then I texted her explaining my diagnosis. She texted me back stating that my great grandmother on her father's side of the family was the only person she knew with breast cancer. Later I would learn that my great grandmother lost her battle to cancer.

I went home and told my mother. My mother was in shock and was trying to process the information piece by piece. She saw me as strong and someone that could handle anything life handed me. But in this moment, she saw the little girl who needed her mother. I kneeled on the floor and put my head on her lap. I don't remember crying but just taking that moment to seek comfort from my mother, to know I was okay and we were going to be okay. I felt that this battle was not just about fighting for myself, but it was also about my promise to take care of her.

I trusted God and I knew He would never forsake me, that He had plans for me, and He promised me life and more abundantly. I knew all these things but I could not understand why he wanted this journey for me. I would repeatedly touch the mass hoping it would disappear and being scared there was something I was doing to make the cancer spread. I began to google everything I could find about stage three breast cancer to be prepared for my meeting with the breast surgeon. I had confirmed in my mind again that this was a faith walk and God wanted me to march out this journey. I prayed and believed that the cancer did not travel to my lymph nodes, I would only need radiation and the surgery would remove the cancerous cyst. What the breast surgeon would tell me would not be outside of this! God is good! He is amazing! He loves me!

That following Monday I confidently made my appointment with the breast cancer surgeon. I was able to see her that Thursday. Leading up to that appointment I did everything I could do to prepare. I got my hair straightened, got my nails done; and purchased a new sun dress. I was prayed up, sacred, blessed and sanctified. I read my bible and knew I was ready for such a time as this. I was going to the appointment alone because I knew I could do this alone; I could do hard things. I would walk boldly knowing that He is God and because of Him I am Ray Janeen Stevens a child of the most High. I remember pulling up in the parking lot of my breast surgeons office and as I parked the song, "Through the Storm" by Yolanda Adams began to play on the radio.

"The storms of life will blow
They're sure to come and go
They meet us all at a time
When I'm calm and doing fine

But the Captain of my soul

He's always on board

He rocks me in His arms

While riding through the storm

While riding through the storm

Jesus holds me in His arms

I am not afraid

Of the stormy winds and the waves

Though the tides become high

He holds me while I ride

I found safety in His arms

While riding through the storm

I have no fear of the raging seas

Knowing Jesus is there with me

He can speak to the wind and the waves

And make them behave

All power's in His hand

On sea or dry land

I found safety in the Master's arms

While riding through the storm

While riding through the storm

Jesus holds me in His arms

No I'm not afraid

Of the stormy wind and the waves

Though the tides become high

He holds me while I ride

I find safety in the Master's arms
While riding through the storm
While riding through the, the storm
While I'm riding through the, the storm
Yeah, while I'm riding through the storm
Jesus holds me in His arms
While I'm riding through the storm
Let the winds blow
I don't care I'm riding through the storm with Jesus
Let the rains fall down
I'm riding through the storm with Jesus
Jesus is the captain of my soul, yes
He is Jesus, the Captain of my soul
I love Him, I love Him, I love Him
I love Him"[6]

    I had never heard this song before but the words were everything I needed at that moment. I broke down in tears and felt with everything in me that God was going to carry me through the storm and this was His confirmation. My truth: although I knew He would carry me through I still did not want to brave the elements of this storm.

---

[6] *"Through the Storm" by Yolanda Adams*

Chapter 4
Damn the Storm

"Trust in the Lord with all your heart, and do not lean on your own understanding." [7]

---

[7] *Proverbs 3:5 NKJV*

As I arrived for my appointment with the breast surgeon, I entered the room with Godfidence. I already knew in my mind my treatment plan, radiation and of course surgery to remove the cancerous cyst. I was ready. I glided in with my dress flowing in the background and my hair was cascading past my shoulders. I proudly announced myself.

"I'm Ray Janeen Stevens here for my 3 o'clock appointment, where do I sign in?"

The receptionist directed me to the sign in form, took my information and told me they would be with me shortly. I remember floating across the floor to my seat awaiting the moment my faith would be proven true and I would be awarded with what I knew would be my preferred treatment plan.

When I was called to the back to speak with the breast surgeon, I was first met by the nurse who took my vitals. I remember ministering to her about the goodness of God and the importance of faith. She said that she admired the way I was responding to the diagnosis and that I was an inspiration. She took off a bracelet she had on her arm - it had charms of little elephants and gave it to me for good luck. I hugged, thanked and told her,

"God is good! He is the same God."

The breast surgeon came into the room and greeted me. She asked me to step down from the observation recliner and come sit next to her, she pulled up a chair. I complied and began to tell her that I made peace with getting radiation and having surgery to remove the cancerous cyst. She told me I was diagnosed with triple negative breast cancer.

"That's good, right? Three negatives make a positive."

She shook her head no. She began to tell me that triple negative breast cancer is one of the most aggressive forms of breast cancer. She told me that radiation will not be an operative treatment plan for the type of cancer I have, but there is another option which is chemotherapy. I asked her if I would lose my hair and she said,

"All your hair."

It was as if she said it in slow motion. All the kumbaya and positive energy I had upon entering this office left. I went from Ray to Ray Ray in thirty seconds. I remember her assistants coming in the room to make sure the doctor was okay. I remember saying,

"Forget her, what about me!?"

This was not one of my proudest moments but it's real. She began to tell me about my next steps and future appointments with her, the reconstructive surgeon, oncologist; genetic counselor; oncology gynecologist, and radiologist for the fine needle biopsy of my breast and lymph node biopsy among other future appointments. I was not ready for this; I was not ready. I felt overwhelmed, anxious, unprepared and alone.

Instead of going home I went to a nearby park and started to do what we are told to never do and that's google a diagnosis. During my search I found that *Triple-negative breast cancer* is a kind of breast cancer that does not have any of the receptors that are commonly found in breast cancer.

The Center for Disease Control and Prevention provides this example:

Think of a cancer cell as a house. The front door may have three kinds of locks, called *receptors*—

To get inside to destroy the cancer, we must bypass three locks on the front door: estrogen, progesterone, and HER2.

If your cancer tests positive for these three locks, which are known as *receptors,* then doctors have a few keys they can use to get inside the cell to destroy it.

Having triple-negative breast cancer, it means those three locks aren't there. So, doctors have fewer keys for treatment. Fortunately, chemotherapy is still an effective option.[8]

After I calmed down, she began to tell me the side effects of chemotherapy. Which are and not limited to,

Hair Loss- I would lose my hair within about two to four weeks of starting chemotherapy. New treatments may help with hair loss, so ask your doctor about that if it's a big concern for you. Your hair will grow back starting around four to six weeks after your last chemotherapy treatment.

Nausea - I would probably feel sick and exhausted for a day or two after each chemotherapy treatment. Queasiness can be treated with a prescription provided by treating physician.

---

[8] *https://www.cdc.gov/cancer/breast/triple-negative.htm*

Fatigue - I may feel tired or have a problem with thinking or remembering things after chemo and radiation therapy. Most of these side effects may go away a few weeks after therapy ends.

Lymphedema - If I have lymph nodes removed during surgery, or if I receive radiation treatment to my lymph nodes, the lymph fluid may not be able to drain properly. This may cause the fluid to build up under my skin and cause part of my body to swell. This condition is called lymphedema.

As per Living Beyond Breast Cancer, in general, about 91% of all women with triple-negative breast cancer are still alive 5 years after diagnosis. [9] If the cancer has spread to the lymph nodes near the breast region the 5-year relative survival rate is about 65%. If the cancer has spread to distant places, the 5-year relative survival rate is 12%. I also found that triple - negative breast cancer was more deadly for African American women. Among women with triple- negative breast cancer, the researchers found African Americans had a 28% increased risk of death.

My breast cancer surgeon told me that triple -negative cancers are more common in patients with hereditary genetic mutations, and genetic counseling and testing should be considered. Because of this I was recommended to see a genetic counselor. A genetic counselor is someone who talks to you about any history of cancer in your family to find out if you have

---

[9] *https://www.lbbc.org/about-us*

a higher risk for getting breast cancer. For example, African American women or people of the Ashkenazi Jewish heritage have a higher risk of inherited genetic changes (mutations) that may cause breast cancers, including triple-negative breast cancer.

If you have a higher risk of getting breast cancer, your doctor may talk about ways to manage your risk. You may also have a higher risk of getting other cancers such as ovarian cancer, and your family may have a higher risk. Children of women with the BRCA mutations who are conceived naturally will have about a 50% risk of inheriting the mutations.

I met with a genetic counselor and found that I indeed tested positive for the BRCA 2 gene. I was told I had a chance of getting ovarian and pancreatic cancer. I had some decisions to make and having a hysterectomy was now added to that list. Being adopted I always wanted children that looked like me and now the opportunity to have children would be taken from me. I felt cheated and overwhelmed.

No one told me about the trauma associated with immediate menopause. According to the Centers for Disease Control and Prevention, the emotional effects can be especially devastating for someone experiencing sudden menopause and can affect your mood and well-being. It can also trigger some uncomfortable symptoms, such as depression, fatigue and hot flashes.

Within a month I would find out I could lose my hair, lose my breast, the ability to have children; possibly my job, my home and the ability to care for my mother. Everyone was telling me they admired my strength but they had no idea my cost. I was physically, emotionally and spiritually drained. I wondered for the first time if I would be ok. Would I lose everything including my life or the ability to take care of my elderly mother?

This was traumatic for me. I could not explain my emotions or feelings into words. My doctor mentioned that some women experience post-traumatic stress disorders, commonly mentioned as PTSD. I learned that this disorder is anxiety driven and developed after experiencing a frightening or life-threatening situation. PTSD is most often referred to in situations such as living through war, a sexual or physical attack, abuse, or a serious accident. Cancer and cancer treatment can also induce PTSD. For example, one study shows that nearly 1 in 4 women who had recently been told they have breast cancer had PTSD.[10] You may develop PTSD from cancer for several reasons. These include:

- Learning you have cancer
- Having pain or other physical problems caused by cancer
- Getting tests and treatments
- Receiving upsetting test results

---

[10] *https://www.cancer.org/treatment/survivorship-during-and-after-treatment/long-term-health-concerns/post-traumatic-stress-disorder-and-cancer.html*

- Long hospital stays or treatments
- The cancer's return or fear of its return [11]

After my appointment with my breast surgeon and the days to follow I would be overwhelmed with doctor appointments. I remember immediately starting to live a lie and pretending that I was okay because I didn't feel like a person with cancer. I did not look sick. I began to ignore every call that came to me from MD Anderson Cancer Center. The breast surgeon wanted to schedule me immediately for my fine needle biopsy of my breast. I ignored the calls from her scheduler because I was not ready to make these decisions alone. I did not have a prepared will, this is requested prior to surgeries. Everything I knew was about to change and I just was not ready to face this storm.

A week later I received a call from MD Anderson Cancer Center from a woman encouraging me to schedule my appointment for my lymph node dissection to see if the cancer had spread to other areas of my body. She explained to me the importance of having the test done as soon as possible due the aggressive nature of the cancer I was diagnosed with and that the sooner I was tested I could begin treatment. She reminded me that God has plans for my life and He would not leave me or forsake me. She was also a cancer survivor and understood my

---

[11] https://www.cancer.net/survivorship/dealing-with-cancer-comes-back

fears and concerns. Her voice was calming and I knew from that conversation she was assigned to my journey. Antoinette was a divine appointment and was present from the beginning until the end of my cancer walk.

After calming my fears, I researched and found that a needle biopsy involves inserting a needle into a lymph node. This type of biopsy can be performed by a radiologist with local anesthesia, using ultrasound or CT scan to find the node. In most cases, there are one to five sentinel nodes, and all are removed. The sentinel nodes are sent to a pathologist to examine under a microscope for signs of cancer. In some cases, sentinel node biopsy is done at the same time as surgery to remove the cancer. Lymph nodes deep in the body cannot be felt or seen. Doctors may use scans or other imaging tests to look for enlarged nodes that are deep in the body. Often, enlarged lymph nodes near a cancer are assumed to contain cancer. Having all the lymph nodes removed can cause some long-term side effects.

Lymph nodes drain fluid from your arms and legs. If the surgeon removed the lymph nodes, fluid could build up and cause swelling in your arms and legs. This is called lymphedema.

Seven days after my lymph node biopsy I received the call that the cancer did not spread to my lymph nodes. I was thankful but knew there were still more tests and decisions to come.

My next appointment was with a reconstructive breast surgeon. My biological mother came with me to this appointment. The breast surgeon explained all of my options. My decision was based on my having the BRCA gene, history of cancer in my family and triple-negative breast cancer. I made the decision of having a double mastectomy because I could not bear going through this again. I chose the option of having DIEP flap surgery which is cutting fat, skin, and blood vessels from the wall of the lower belly and relocating it to the chest to rebuild your chest. One major advantage of the DIEP Flap procedure is the preservation of abdominal muscle function and strength. The fat and vessels are harvested, shaped, and transferred to the chest. The vessels are then reconnected using microsurgical techniques to create natural appearing breasts. [12]

I wanted to make sure that I did everything in my power to prevent recurrence. It's amazing how prior to this point I did not put heavy focus on my breast but in that moment, I felt as if I was losing a part of me that was "mine." I felt robbed and I felt alone.

Once my appointment came to an end, my biological mother asked if she could hug me, which was different from our previous interactions. I told her,

"Yes."

---

[12] *https://www.orlandohealth.com/content-hub/breast-reconstruction-after-mastectomy-advantages-of-the-diep-flap-procedure*

She asked if I was going to be okay and I told her yes. She told me she loved me as she hugged me and then left for work. I went back upstairs to the waiting area and sat to process everything. I needed to be at work soon but I was mentally and emotionally drained and I was yearning for comfort. I was scared and overwhelmed.

While sitting in the waiting area I made eye contact with a woman who sat directly across from me. I would learn her name was Joyce. She asked me, "are you ok?" This was first time my eyes filled with water and the tears began to flow with no words to follow. There weren't words to describe the emotions I was feeling. While she was there for her own appointment she began to pray for and encourage me. She asked me where and when my surgery was scheduled. I gave Joyce my information and thanked her for "seeing" me. She was like an angel that was placed in that exact moment just for me. As God would have it, I would see her again.

That day while at work I had multiple conversations with God trying to process my next steps. I had silent prayer asking Him for confidence over my decisions and faith to accept the new season and plans He had for me. I was honest with God about my fears and for the first time in my life, I felt anxious and depressed. Although I was going through a difficult season, I was conscious of making sure my mother did not feel or see any concern that I had during this time.

Later that week as I had done previously, I would stop at a local park on my way home from work to gather my thoughts. On this particular day I parked and started looking through Facebook and ran across a post from someone who generally would post about her "waking up and shimmering," making a difference in the world, or being a light to others. She had an organization called "Carie Cares" and was always seeking ways to make a difference in the life of others. When reading her post it moved me to tears. She wrote that she loves God and every day she is intentional about fighting the depression she faces based on the loss of her precious son due to addiction. Her honesty and transparency touched me and opened the door for me to be honest with myself and my feelings. She wrote that everyone expected her to be upbeat but today was hard and she fights every day to keep going. I commented on her post, thanking her for being obedient and posting this as it may have been for her, it was also for me.

Carie began supporting my cancer journey in so many ways. She had and still tends her garden where she grows herbs to make natural products for healing. On any given day she would make and bring different variations of lotion, oils, and lip balm to assist with healing from chemotherapy and surgeries. Not only would she bring fresh herbs produced from her garden but she would encourage me to be an advocate for my own care by teaching me to make my own products. One gift I have to this day is of a wishing necklace that she prayed over. I wore this

necklace during every chemotherapy appointment. Today Carie
and I are chosen sisters and although I thought our connection
would be for a time such as this, God had other plans. She
would teach me about grief and the ability to move forward
during unimaginable loss.

During this time, I learned so much about prayer and the
importance of seeking God in all things. Although things were
overwhelming for me, they were not for Him. I saw that each
time I consulted with Him and was honest about my feelings,
provision was made through people that were able to see me
despite their current circumstance. I did not know the outcome or
what was next, I did know and felt God's presence and He would
remain with me. I knew I was in the process of activating my
faith and divine appointments were being put in place to further
assist. Faith becomes active and effective when it is built on a
strong foundation. Trusting the unknown and unseen, believing
in God's word and His promises, trusting His word,
acknowledging his miraculous works and repeating his promises
activates my faith.

God works through our lives by divine appointments and
I knew Antoinette, Joyce and Carie were mine. Much of the time
we live, we're unconscious of God at work moving and
intervening. It is quite possible that God sends us divine
appointments every day and we miss them because we aren't
looking for them. Far too often what is really God moving and
intervening in the midst of life is written off as coincidence.

There are divine appointments God sets for each of our lives and the possibilities of them are endless. If you are willing to be led by the Holy Spirit, great things are possible. God has shown me the importance of waiting on Him as He will manifest His mercy and grace through the divine appointments He has sent.

Chapter 5
Waiting On God

"But they who wait for the Lord shall renew their strength; they shall mount up with wings like eagles; they shall run and not be weary; they shall walk and not faint." [13]

---

[13] *Isaiah 40:31 KJV*

Due to the aggressive nature of my breast cancer diagnosis, it was insisted that I have a PET scan and fine needle biopsy. Doctors use diagnostic tests like biopsies and imaging exams to determine a cancer's grade and its stage.[14] I was told that my provider would place the needle directly into the biopsy site or through a small incision and remove a sample of the tissue or fluid. I may feel pressure when the sample is taken and pressure would be applied to the biopsy site until the bleeding stopped.

Knowing what to expect I knew I needed time off from work. My prior doctor appointments were made either before work or on my scheduled day off. My appointment for the fine needle biopsy could only be made during working hours. I remember telling the person who oversaw my schedule and my supervisor at work that I needed to be two hours late due to a previously scheduled doctor's appointment. At first I was hesitant because I was still under my 90-day probationary period, but I was given the approval to come to work late on this particular day.

I arrived at the appointment nervous about the biopsy. I had just completed a positron emission tomography scan (PET Scan), which is an imaging test that uses a radioactive substance called a tracer, to look for potential spread of breast cancer. This

---

[14] *https://www.mdanderson.org/patients-family/diagnosis-treatment/a-new-diagnosis/cancer-grade-vs--cancer-stage.html*

tracer can help identify areas of cancer that an MRI or CT scan may not show.[15]

This needle biopsy was painful and caused bleeding, bruising, and swelling. I was given an ice pack to place on my breast throughout the remainder of the day. After the biopsy I was exhausted but this feeling was becoming my new norm. I was told to take some time to sit and rest before leaving the appointment but my focus was on getting to work to complete my day. I did not want anyone to know I had breast cancer; I need this job more than ever now.

When I arrived at work I was met by a coworker, Kim, who I became friendly with during my time at the company. She gave me a heads up that my name was listed as a "No Show" for the day. I explained I received prior approval to have a late start due to a doctor's appointment I had previously scheduled. The person who gave me the approval had left to go back to the Maryland office and I had a gut feeling about what was about to happen.

I sat in the common area feeling defeated, knowing that I had done all I could do. Kim asked me to wait while she went to get someone to speak with me. While she was gone, I sat and completely disconnected from every distraction around me. I closed my eyes and began praying to my God. I had a real, transparent conversation with my Father. I told God that I was tired and I've done all I know to do. I was scared and I needed to

---

[15] *https://medlineplus.gov/ency/article/007469.htm*

give this all to Him because I could not do this on my own strength. I needed Him and I couldn't carry this anymore. I've worked so hard and I've fought to trust this process but I don't know what to do now. God, what do I do if I don't have a job or medical insurance? I asked for His will to be done and I surrendered all.

At that moment, my coworker told me a woman named Melanie would come out to speak with me. I waited for maybe five minutes and then Kim and Melanie walked up to me. Melanie's title was Senior Analyst of Communication and Employee Engagement. She asked me to come with her to a conference room. I followed thinking this was the end of my employment with this company. While walking into the conference room I remember it being cold and I was emotionally numb. Kim was also with us and she sat beside Melanie.

I began telling my story of my diagnosis and all that had taken place up to that point. I explained that I had just returned from having a breast biopsy and I was unable to get an appointment prior to my start time. As I was talking to Melanie, I saw her eyes fill with tears. She was looking at my breast and unbeknownst to me I did not know there was dried blood that had come through my bandage through my shirt. I began to tell more of my journey and as I did I knew she saw me in this moment. After talking more and detailing my journey she instructed me to go home and rest. I felt a peace come over me and I knew it was God.

From that moment, the approval process for my disability and paid time off from work had begun. I would have close to a year off from work for all of my tests, surgeries, chemotherapy treatments, and appointments. I had time to finally process my diagnosis and put a plan in place to fight for my life while being present to care for my mother.

I asked Melanie what made her come out of her office to speak with me. She told me that she had a lot of tasks that day and was not going to come meet with me because her colleague oversaw my area. However, there was something urging her to speak with me. Today we know that to be the Holy Spirit. I'm so thankful that she allowed God to lead her that day. At present I am a $800,000 cancer patient with no medical debt. As I reflect, I know that by resigning from the nonprofit I worked for in 2013, walking in faith and taking the path designed by God, I am able to say this today. I could have lost everything...But God. Today Melanie is president of my 501(C)(3) *And What If You Live?* I am so thankful that Melanie holds a key role in my purpose and ministry. God hand-picked her for my divine appointment and I am forever grateful.

Unfortunately, between 20 and 30 percent of women diagnosed with breast cancer will lose their jobs. Working women who survive breast cancer are significantly more likely to lose their jobs, according to a new study.[16]

---

[16] https://www.statnews.com/2017/02/06/poor-women-lose-jobs-cancer/

Many people are forced to take time off while getting chemotherapy treatment to deal with extreme fatigue, nausea and other immediate side effects of the therapy. The researchers say it's possible this could lead to long-term employment problems for a number of reasons. For example, chemotherapy treatments can cause long-term side effects such as neuropathy or cognitive issues, causing a drop-off in work performance.[17]

One study from the American Cancer Society found that cancer survivors who had less than 1 year of financial reserves had a reduced quality of life and more trouble from symptoms than those who had reserves. Other studies show people with cancer are more likely to declare bankruptcy than similar people without a cancer history. And those cancer patients who declared bankruptcy, also have an increased risk of death compared with cancer patients who haven't declared it.

I feared potential financial problems would make me less recommended for treatment. Would I need to make tradeoffs between cancer treatment, housing or food for me and my mother? Will my breast cancer worsen my health from stress? Who will care for my mother? Who will take care of me? The stress of wondering and not knowing took me to a place of extreme anxiety. If I felt this, there had to be countless others that were going through the same emotional rollercoaster. Research now suggests that chronic stress can actually make cancer spread faster. Stress can speed up the spread of cancer

---

[17] *https://www.cancer.net/survivorship/long-term-side-effects-cancer-treatment*

throughout the body, especially in ovarian, breast and colorectal cancer. When the body becomes stressed, neurotransmitters like norepinephrine are released, which stimulate cancer cells.[18] I was trying to care for my mother the same way I did prior to my diagnosis. I thought this would make her comfortable seeing me keeping my same routine of caregiving. I would become fatigued from trying to meet the daily demands of appointments, tests and caring for my mother. It happened so suddenly but I noticed a change in my energy level.

Cancer-related fatigue (CRF, sometimes simply called "cancer fatigue") is one of the most common side effects of cancer and its treatments. Many people who are chronically ill feel tired. But cancer-related fatigue goes beyond the usual tiredness. People who experience cancer fatigue often describe it as "paralyzing." Usually, it comes on suddenly and is not the result of activity or exertion. With this type of fatigue, no amount of rest or sleep helps. You feel physically, emotionally and mentally exhausted most of the time. Cancer related fatigue affects 80% to 100% of people with cancer. Stress can worsen feelings of fatigue.[19] This can include any type of stress, from dealing with the disease and the unknowns to worrying about daily accomplishments or worrying about not meeting the expectations of others.

---

[18] https://www.cityofhope.org/living-well/is-there-a-connection-between-chronic-stress-and-cancer
[19] https://my.clevelandclinic.org/health/diseases/5230-cancer-fatigue

I know that in an instance I could have lost everything and that any of these scenarios could have been my testimony. Through this part of my journey, I learned about the power of prayer and waiting on God for direction and resolution.

"But those who wait on the Lord Shall renew their strength; They shall mount up with wings like eagles, they shall run and not be weary, they shall walk and not faint" [20]

Moving forward it would become even more evident that I needed to not only wait on God but trust His promises through disappointments and dreams deferred.

---

[20] *Isaiah 40:31 ESV*

Chapter 6
My Daughter - A Dream Deferred Not Forgotten

"He gives the barren woman a home, making her the joyous mother of children." [21]

---

[21] Psalms 113:9 ESV

My surgery was quickly approaching for my double mastectomy and DIEP flap surgery. My doctor decided it was best for me to have the surgery to remove the cancerous cyst prior to beginning chemotherapy. The surgery was scheduled the day after Labor Day and instead of resting or attending a cookout, I spent the day cleaning my home. With everything I was facing, all I could think about was making sure my home was clean and my mom saw me "in control."

Prior to scheduling my initial surgery, I was asked if I had a will. At that moment I became paralyzed because my initial thought was death. This made everything become too real for me. I was told that not only would I need a will or living trust, but also an Advance Care Directive, a Health Care Proxy and Durable power of attorney. My attorney had drafted my documents and in true fashion, I waited until the day before my surgery to have a neighbor sign as witness on the forms. I waited until the last minute because just the thought of creating a will made me anxious. I did not want to consider my demise or not being alive and well to take care of my mother.

That evening Danny, my biological father, was expected to arrive from Sharon, PA. I had not seen him in almost 25 years. When I called to tell him about my diagnosis, he immediately said he was coming to support me. There was something about having him come that made the little girl in me feel safe. I had lost my adoptive father in 2006 to lung cancer and it was so difficult not having him here to support me. Now more than ever, I experienced the absence of his love, sense of security and safety that he always provided to me.

When Danny arrived that evening, it was as if no time had passed. My mother and my biological father seemed to talk more than we did, realizing that both their birthdays were October 17th. Cindy, my close sister friend, arrived to spend the night as she was driving me to my surgery the following morning. As I look back on that night, I remember sitting in the distance thinking about the world wind that had happened in six weeks and dreams I had that were deferred.

I began to think about my wait for the perfect time to have a child. I wanted to wait until I finished college, until I had the perfect job, marriage and home. At this moment none of this seemed important. Has God forgotten about me and my dreams? Instantly I learned that time waits for no one and that after this surgery I had to prepare for my hysterectomy and having a biological child of my own would no longer be possible.

As I considered that I was a carrier of the BRCA gene, I realized that if I were to have a child, I could very well give this gene to my them. Fighting for my life was one thing but watching my child go through this and knowing the gene was passed from me would have been devastating.

Arriving at the hospital the following morning I had and felt tremendous love and support. I was so grateful to see my former Executive Director and dear friend Bernetta who came to support me. My church family and dear friend Erica made sure I was spiritually prepared for the surgery. Ms. Mumford, a friend of my mothers and a member of our church, led us into prayer and prayed over my surgeons. My biological grandmother, mother and father were there to support me and my dear mother and big sister Cindy never left my side. I felt God's presence and knew He was with me. As I entered the surgical room and began to count backwards, I told God that I trusted His plans for me.

The surgery for my double mastectomy and DIEP flap surgery lasted 16 hours. I was awakened in recovery sometime after 1:00am with a breathing tube in my throat. It was the most uncomfortable feeling to experience. I heard my mother's voice and the nurse read a letter from my friends and loved ones that had stayed the duration of my surgery. Several made their way to see me and to let me know they were present and never left me.

Later that afternoon I was brought to my room. My mom, biological father, Cindy and close friends were waiting for me. I was in my room for a little over an hour when a familiar face walked through the door. I looked up and saw Joyce from the waiting area at MD Anderson that prayed for me. She remembered my surgery date and wanted to make sure I knew I was not alone and that God was the same God. Joyce is still in my life today and I call her Aunt Joyce. Since meeting, we've supported each other through illness and loss. Joyce was and is my divine appointment.

The next morning, I woke up in my hospital bed with my head facing the window. The early morning sun was coming through the blinds. I felt a warmth, a feeling of peace beyond all understanding. I was connected to a machine to give me morphine on demand; IV's and drains were attached to my body. I heard the door to my hospital room open and as the person entered my room I clearly heard a voice say to me,

"Tell them that I said they were going to be okay."

Sight unseen with my head facing the window I said to this person,

"Honey, I don't know what you are going through but God wanted me to tell you that you are going to be okay."

As I turned my head to face this person, I saw a beautiful young lady with tears in her eyes and sadness in her spirit. I asked her to hold my hand and told her that I "saw" her.

I later learned that she worked in housekeeping and was there that morning to clean my room. For the entirety of my stay at the hospital, I saw her. She would make my room her last to clean so that she could sit and talk with me. I knew God was doing something but I was unsure as to His plan. I was obedient and took this time to sow into her and speak life. She would sit by my bed and listen, hanging on to every word.

The day I left the hospital I had her write her name and number on this bright yellow notepad I had brought with me. I promised her that I would keep in touch with her and I did.

Today I am so grateful to say that she has been in my life for the past 7 years and calls me "mom." I could not have asked for a better daughter. Parts of me will live on through her. She has seen firsthand how God allowed me to navigate through my diagnosis and life changes, she is an extension of who I am. Christmas 2021 she gave me a card that read,

"You are one of my favorite gifts from God. It's me and you always. You are a great mother."

She is my perfect daughter and God blessed my entire life when she entered it. I had a plan for what giving birth looked like for me, but God had His own plan for my life. He still gave me the desires of my heart, my daughter with big, beautiful eyes. My daughter showed me that God had not forgotten about me. He gave me a divine appointment that I will cherish until the day He calls me home. I love her so much.

I am thankful for this beautiful gift of love and light, however I still looked for self-acceptance for the new version of me. I realized I needed to begin the process of loving myself and walking with confidence. Despite everything I was still God's masterpiece. Right?

Chapter 7
Still His Masterpiece

"For we are God's masterpiece. He has created us anew in Christ Jesus, so we can do the good things He planned for us long ago."[22]

---

[22] *Ephesians 2:10 NLT*

After my surgery I returned home to recover and heal. I was fully aware that there was more ahead and I needed to be prepared for what was to come. When you go through a diagnosis of any kind the same responsibility, issues and concerns you had prior are still prominent. After being released from the hospital I came home to my mother who still had her same needs and depended on me to make decisions for her and our home. The bills still needed to be paid, my mother needed to be fed, groceries picked up, her appointments made and the house cleaned. My mother also needed to know that she was seen, heard and still in a safe place to be taken care of by me. My mother's wellbeing would be a major concern for me throughout my cancer journey.

My mother and I were blessed to have the support of her dear friends, Ms. Norman, Mr. Fleming, Ms. Freison, Ms. Wall, Ms. Mumford and our church community. Her friends ensured that she kept all of her doctor appointments and attended church. However, I still felt overwhelmed with caring for her and managing my self-care and healing. I was caregiving while needing a caregiver. There were times I felt unseen and unheard. If I screamed would anyone hear me? People would say that I was so strong but they did not see me or know my cost. Breast cancer made me a part of a world I did not want to be included in and although I did not want to be a victim, I felt like I was held captive, released by my hostages and every day I was waiting for my captives to return.

As I prepared for chemotherapy, I tried to make peace with what was to come. I was blessed to have Cindy who I lovingly call "big sis" volunteer to take me to all of my appointments. She had just retired and said she wanted to do this for me. The fact that she drove from Philadelphia to my home in New Jersey every other week, picked me up and sat with me during treatments meant the world to me. We would leave early enough to have breakfast at one of our favorite diners because we knew that for days to follow, I would not be able to eat or keep any food down. When it was difficult for me to speak for myself Cindy became my advocate. She would keep notes from all of my appointments and make sure to ask questions that I may have missed. There were times I knew she was tired but didn't want me to know. To this day there is not a conversation I end with her that I do not tell her she is loved. I will never forget what she did for me and how she supported me with unconditional love.

I was given a date to get my port, which is a device used to give chemotherapy treatments. Instead of getting a port placed under my skin, I was told that I would start my treatments that day and I would get treatment through a vein. They began to insert the needle through a vein in my hand since my veins are smaller and hidden. I'm genetically predisposed to having problematic veins. This was painful and when using the saline flush which is a mixture of salt and water to push the chemotherapy through the IV line into my vein, I felt an overwhelming burning sensation.

I would return home exhausted from the treatment and feel a range of emotions. I did my research and prepared for side effects but nothing prepared me for how I felt and what was to come proceeding my treatment. The first week I had weakness, nausea and lack of appetite but I still had my hair. I thought that I would be the exception and my hair would stay intact.

I researched the cold cap method which are cold caps that are frozen devices intended to decrease the risk of hair loss from chemotherapy treatments. The cold temperature is to decrease blood flow to your scalp, thereby preventing chemotherapy drugs from affecting your hair follicles. In theory, by preserving your hair follicles, you may be able to prevent significant hair loss. I was excited and purchased the cold cap but unfortunately it did not work. After my second chemotherapy treatment my hair started to come out in clumps.

I remember waking up on a Monday morning and seeing strands of hair on my pillowcase. I went into the bathroom and began combing my hair and seeing a sink full of hair. It did not take much for my hair to come out, I just ran my fingers through my scalp and my hair came out instantaneously. As women, hair loss is a very real concern. Because hair can be so strongly tied to not only our perception of ourselves but to our femininity; hair loss can be devastating and sudden hair loss can cause trauma. Everyone responds to chemotherapy in different ways. You could lose your hair, it may become thinner, or it's possible you'll keep all of your hair. If you do lose your hair, expect it to start one to three weeks after your first chemotherapy treatment. This proved true for me.

I called a friend who worked at a salon and I told her my hair was coming out and I needed her to shave my head. That afternoon I met her to try on some wigs and unbeknownst to me she had planned to bless me by purchasing my first wig. After returning to my house and trying on the wigs she began the process of shaving my head. With tears in my eyes I precisely remember asking her to keep my sideburns so that when I wore a baseball cap it would look as if I had hair underneath my hat. When washing my face, I was intentional to not wash my sideburns. I tried to keep them as long as possible which was only two additional weeks. As I am writing, I still cannot believe the measures I took to hold on to every strand of my hair to look normal.

My good friend expressed that the hair loss was almost worse than dealing with the cancer itself. For her, every time someone asked her about the hair loss, she had to relive the pain of coping with cancer. As a strong woman coping daily with her disease, she found that providing the explanation and seeing the look of sadness and awkwardness of others made her become even more self-conscious and I couldn't agree with her more. I did not feel attractive and going out in public made me anxious. I felt awkward and it did not matter what anyone told me it did not change the way I saw myself or the way I began to treat myself.

People asked me how I was able to care for my mother while going through chemotherapy treatment and my answer remains the same today. It was easier for me to show up for her because I could not show up for myself. I was too exhausted and depressed to do the things that in the past were so natural for me like bathe, brush my teeth, pray, take vitamins and medication. But for my mother, I was able to be there for her and make sure she was taken care of because in that season I loved her but not me. My body had betrayed me and I had not forgiven it. I equate this to having your spouse turn their back on you and leave you without an explanation. You are left to grieve the relationship while the world goes on. Everyone expects you to carry on as normal but you are left with the memories of what was and may never be again. I felt an expectation to pick up the pieces and carry on although I was broken.

Even though I was sick, my mother still perceived that I was strong and okay. I think she saw this because she needed to and the alternative would have been too much for her to bear. My mother had a difficult childhood after losing her mother at the age of six. She moved from home to home or as she put it "pillar to post" during all of her youth. She did not meet and marry my father until her late 30's and from their union wanted to give love to children like her by fostering. Little did she know she would adopt the first two children that came into her home.

In my lifetime I've made many promises that I remember and have proudly kept. Prior to my father taking his last breath I promised him that he could go rest because I would take care of my mother. I needed to fulfill my promise.

When experiencing a diagnosis of any kind we are forced to deal not only with the diagnosis but every issue. There is hurt, insecurity, doubt, failed relationships, daily responsibility and life disappointment we navigate prior to the diagnosis. I was not the same person but everyone was treating me like I was and in some strange way, although I resented this, I needed to believe it to survive.

On January 8th, 2016, the day after my 45th birthday I had my last chemotherapy appointment and was to ring the bell. I was so thankful Cindy was there with me. I walked in preparing to have my IV inserted for the last time and intentionally looked at everyone within eyesight getting their treatment because I was yearning to feel something. I heard from the nurses that this was an exciting day for me but my truth was that I felt nothing. I felt so guilty about not feeling the emotions I was expected to feel while countless others wish they could be in my position.

When I was diagnosed with cancer I was forced and knew how to fight. I was provided with daily tasks and a medical plan. After ringing the bell no one told me what was next. After going through this trauma no one gave me a plan on what to do to stay healthy mentally, physically and spiritually. It was like I was being sent off to war with no weapons or armor. I was uncertain about recurrence, the new me and fully knowing who that was because to me she was lost. I did not know how to live.

After chemotherapy treatments I found myself becoming more forgetful than normal. I could not remember dates, names and things I would generally know at any given time. I learned that many people experience mental changes after chemotherapy treatment. This is sometimes called "chemo brain." Some may have problems such as poor memory, trouble finding words, or difficulty focusing. This affected many aspects of my life, including caring for my mother and managing my job.

I found that keeping a calendar, writing everything down, and exercising my brain with puzzles and reading helped me. It was important for me to focus on one task at a time. Most people say it takes six to twelve months after they finish chemotherapy before they truly feel like themselves again.

After chemotherapy was completed, it was time for me to schedule my breast revision, hysterectomy and corrective surgery from my DIEP flap surgery. After x-rays it was determined that stomach muscle was cut during my DIEP flap surgery which caused a hernia. The breast reconstructive surgeon and gynecologic cancer surgeon decided to perform both surgeries to correct the hernia and hysterectomy at the same time.

Anticipating the hysterectomy brought emotions of anger, disappointment and finality. I felt cheated of not being able to have a child of my own and as if my femininity was taken from me. During this time and thereafter I would have many incidents when I would feel a hardness or discomfort in both breasts. My first response would be and still is to immediately call my breast surgeon for an MRI. For me, my greatest fear has been knowing the cancer can come back. But the greatest comfort is knowing God is the same God and He promised me life and life more abundant.

"A 2022 systematic review published earlier this year from Cornell University found that the most common unmet need among cancer survivors is calming fear of recurrence. The constant worry often leads to depression, impaired daily functioning, and reduced quality of life. Many cancer survivors worry for years and report that they feel as worried as when they were first diagnosed with cancer. The review combined data from 46 studies with more than 9,000 participants from 13 countries. The studies all used data from the Fear of Cancer Recurrence Inventory, a widely accepted survey to identify clinically significant fear. Nearly 60 percent of study participants had fears that were clinically significant, and nearly 20 percent scored at the highest level, meaning their fear of cancer recurrence was debilitating."[23]

After going through therapy, I also found that my withdrawal from building a relationship with a significant other was based on my fear of not living. Not only was I fearful of a

---

[23] *https://onlinelibrary.wiley.com/doi/pdfdirect/10.1002/pon.5921*

recurrence, but I was also not happy with who I saw when I looked in the mirror. How can a man be pleased with me when I'm not pleased with who I see when I look at myself?

"Body image is one part of self-esteem. Self-esteem is how you feel about yourself as a whole. People with healthy self-esteem generally feel good about themselves and believe they deserve respect from others. Being diagnosed with and treated for breast cancer is one of many experiences that can affect your body image and self-esteem. How you feel about your body image during and after treatment depends on a number of things. For example, your self-esteem and body image can be related to the type of treatment you've had (and how your body may have changed as a result), your personal history, and how you felt about yourself physically and emotionally before cancer." [24]

As for me I had artificial breasts that were uneven with no nipple and a scar the entire width of my stomach from DIEP flap surgery. I had abnormalities as far as my weight fluctuation, not to mention other concerns that would follow.

"Living Beyond Breast Cancer states, "there is no doubt breast cancer treatment can cause trauma that affects your body, your mind, and your emotions. Surgery, chemotherapy, radiation therapy, and other treatments can have side effects that impact how you look and feel; and treatment, in general, can make you

---

[24] *https://www.lbbc.org/about-breast-cancer/wellness-body-image/how-breast-cancer-impacts-your-body-image*

feel tired and scared. It's not unusual to experience depression or anxiety at some point before, during or after treatment." [25]

Throughout this journey I've learned to challenge my negative thoughts. Our minds are powerful and when we feel or think something, we innately believe it to be true. But feelings are not facts. Instead of accepting my thoughts and feelings as the truth, I began to stop and question them. Do I have evidence to prove this feeling or thought to be true? If not, it's just my brain spinning a story.

The more I question my negative thoughts, the easier it will become to separate myself from them. I would learn that it's all about facing the feelings head on and taking away its power. I read that it was important to write myself letters of self-compassion. The idea was to write to yourself from a point in the future looking back on the moment you are in. Imagine, what you would want to hear from your future self and write your response in third person.

I've looked back at the letters I've written to myself and I cried for her because of the pain she was navigating through while fearful of the unknown and her new normal. I would eventually learn to focus on the good and show myself the same level of compassion I would if I were writing to a friend or loved one. I saved these letters to read when I feel down and need a reminder of what God can do in my life despite a diagnosis or life obstacles.

---

[25] *https://www.lbbc.org*

Over time I learned to love all of me. For some time, I could not look at myself because I saw the imperfections of scaring. I thought of the surgeries and the drains and still did not feel prepared to embrace it all. In an effort to force myself to "see" me, I purchased a full-length mirror and a portrait stand to place it on because it was important for me to remind myself that I am God's masterpiece. Today, I encourage others to know that it's important to SEE and ACCEPT yourself with all that you perceive as inadequate.

I am physically not the woman I used to be and my health and aging is a factor but I've learned it's important to be okay with what and who I see in the mirror. The things I can change I will work on and the things I cannot, I will give them to God.

Joel Osteen once wrote "You've been made in the image of God. When you criticize yourself, you are criticizing God's creation. You are saying, God you didn't do too good for me." [26]

No, God wasn't having an off day when He created me. He called me a masterpiece. Self-care is remembering who you are to God. I'm learning every day to let the one who created me to be the one who defines me. God will provide what I need to accept and love me. I was now ready to move forward with my hysterectomy or so I thought.

---

[26] *Joel Osteen*

Chapter 8
Lost and Found

"For the Son of Man came to seek and to save the lost." [27]

---

[27] *Luke 19:10 NLT*

After my double mastectomy, DIEP flap surgery and chemotherapy it was now time for me to prepare for my hysterectomy. The surgery was quick but the mental and physical recovery was long lasting. I felt a sadness and depression that to this day can't be fully expressed by words or emotion.

After the hysterectomy which was done as a precautionary measure due to having the BRCA gene, no one told me the extent of the side effects that I could experience. I felt sadness every day and it was a struggle to think of anything positive as it related to my new normal. I was supposed to be happy to be alive, right? I mean God still has me here and I should be ecstatic to still be amongst the living. My truth? I felt dead inside. I was concerned about keeping my mother's environment secure, and my friends seeing me as the same strong person they knew prior. I struggled with expressing how I truly felt with the thought of being judged and deemed ungrateful.

I felt guilty and often asked God for forgiveness. I couldn't understand how I, being a woman who loved the Lord and believed in his promise for my tomorrow, could carry the disappointment, despair and sadness I did every day. It was as if I was living a double life in every aspect. A few relationships were severed because I was not "seen" and when I could not meet certain expectations and show up in the manner I had in the past, I was no longer needed.

Signs of depression can include one or more of the following: sadness, loss of energy, feelings of hopelessness or worthlessness, loss of enjoyment, difficulty concentrating, uncontrollable crying, difficulty making decisions, irritability, increased need for sleep, insomnia or excessive sleep, a change in appetite causing weight loss or gain, and thoughts of death or suicide or attempting suicide.

I learned that my change in mood was common with surgical menopause. Depression, anxiety, mood swings, and panic attacks were all common in perimenopause and menopause and can often be related to an imbalance between progesterone and estrogen. Menopause affects not only our bodies but our emotions and brain functionality.

"Surgical menopause involves the removal of your ovaries (oophorectomy), either on its own or in conjunction with a hysterectomy. Since the ovaries are your body's main source of estrogen production, this could immediately trigger menopause, regardless of your age." It can affect hot flashes and mood and can increase the rate at which a woman loses bone and may develop osteoporosis. There's a concern that younger women who go into menopause might be at an increased risk of heart disease later in life. It could also affect cognitive function.

It is important to see a physician ahead of time before removal of the ovaries to talk about estrogen replacement therapy."

It was a Wednesday morning and my mother was just picked up to go to the senior program at our church. I remember looking at my mother and thinking that she would be okay if I were not here anymore. I felt exhausted and did not have the energy I had prior along with the mental and emotional capacity to care for her or myself. It's disconcerting how the enemy can use our being mentally and emotionally exhausted as its playground. I felt hopeless and did not anticipate the future. It was then that I called out to God to help me. I got on my knees and asked for Him to clear my mind and help me to see the plans He had for my life. To give me hope as He promised.

"For I know the plans I have for you." says the Lord. They are plans for Good and not for disaster, to give you a future and a hope. In those days when you pray, I will listen. If you look for me wholeheartedly, you will find me."[28]

I felt an immediate calming and peace come over me and knew that He was with me and has never left my side. In the midst of the obstacles we face, He is still God and is waiting for us to seek Him.

After my time with God, I decided to get out of the house and go for a ride. I ended up at my local Wawa for a cup of coffee. There was this kind spirited woman name Tina who was a cashier there and being in her presence would always provide a positive mood shift. Tina was pure light.

---

[28] *Jeremiah 29:11-13 NLT*

As I approached Wawa and got out of my car I saw a woman who looked familiar and upon walking toward her, I realized I did not know her. As I began to walk past her to the door, we spoke to each other and I complimented her on her hair. It was beautiful, natural and big! I remember thinking, God, I sure could use even ten percent of her beautiful hair. I kept trying to figure out if I knew her because there was a familiarity with no explanation. As I exited the Wawa she was still standing there. I am not sure what drove me to tell her about my finishing chemotherapy or not having hair. We started a conversation and she told me she was a life coach and invited me over to her home for dinner. Who does that? To some this might seem odd but today I know that Dena was my divine appointment. We became friends on Facebook, and yes, I did take her up on her invitation for dinner, which was delicious.

I knew Dena saw me, not the version I portrayed to my family and friends but the me that was broken and needed help. We began to keep in touch and our trust and bond grew. I remember the day I admitted to myself that I did not have the tools to fight for the life I wanted. This was the day I called Dena and told her I was ready to do the work to live again. The day I said yes was the day I made the conscious decision to live.

It is one thing to acknowledge the plans God has for us but it is completely another to say yes to His plans and boldly walk in faith. I was not sure what to expect from working with Dena except it would be better than what I was currently doing on my own. I would meet Dena at 6:00 am at a local Chick-Fil-A or a zoom call before work on Saturday mornings. Not only would meeting with her help me identify the issues I needed to face, but would also address the consequences of not dealing with past hurts and rejection prior to my cancer diagnosis. I needed to heal from my past so that I could receive my future.

Dena would prove to not only feed my physical body but also my spiritual and mental life and became my coach. I not only wanted to live for myself but I wanted and needed to heal to help others to do the same. During one of our meetings, I expressed to her my desire to help others going through a life challenge or diagnosis. This was driven off of not wanting other to feel the helplessness I felt and give up too soon before discovering the authority they had to fulfill all God had for their future. Dena asked me,

"Ray Janeen, what is stopping you?"

My truth? After facing death twice in my life, I believed God was keeping me alive to fulfill His purpose and once that purpose was completed, He would call me home. I thought that as long as I just moved in my life with purpose deferred and not completed, He would keep me alive. After surviving my diagnosis, I began to lose so many I held dear and at times my soul felt empty and alone. I asked Dena,

"If I fulfill God's purpose, what if I die?"

And together we said,

"And what if you live?"

Having a coach started me on my healing journey. I also discovered exercise, vitamins and diet played a key role in my overall health. I began to have a consistent workout schedule that included cardio and strength training that helped me physically and emotionally. As per breastcancer.org, regular exercise is an important part of being as healthy after and during a cancer diagnosis. Also, being physically active can reduce your risk of developing breast cancer. If you've been diagnosed with breast cancer, exercise can reduce the risk of the cancer recurrence. Exercise also can help ease troubling treatment side effects, such as fatigue, pain, depression, and lymphedema.

Taking vitamins also helped with the side effects from my treatment and diagnosis. My vitamin regimen consists of Vitamin D 2000 units/day, Calcium with Magnesium 500-600 mg, Omega 3 1000-1500 mg per day, Curcumin 500 mg per day and Probiotics daily of 5-7 strains, which is recommended by my oncologist.

"Vitamin D is a key nutrient for your mental and physical health. Studies have linked low vitamin D levels to depression. Taking vitamin D supplements may help improve depression symptoms. Also, there is a link between the health of your gut, microbiome and hormones. When gut health isn't optimal, hormones become imbalanced. Scientists know that 95% of serotonin is produced and stored in the gut. This is why people with unhealthy microbiomes also often experience feelings of depression and anxiety."[29]

Presently Dena does not know where my mind was that day and that I was ready to leave this earth. This is one thing I never shared with her because speaking this truth made it real. Her obedience to God and inviting me to her home that day helped me to see that God yet again heard my cry and was ever present.

The enemy is the author of confusion and distraction and when we are emotionally and mentally drained, he will come to kill, still and destroy. I am thankful that I knew God that day and the power and promises He had over my life. God saved me that September day and I am forever grateful.

I'm often reminded of the people who are no longer here and lost their journey. There are people who have touched my life and have gone to glory. Sometimes I would softly ask God why he chose to keep me here? I'm so thankful He did but I would still wonder.

---

[29] *https://www.ncbi.nlm.nih.gov/pmc/articles/PMC6970300/*

Chapter 9
Sole Survivor

"The Lord is near to the brokenhearted and saves the crushed in spirit." [30]

---

[30] *Psalms 34:18 AMP*

No one told me about survivor's guilt. "Survivors' guilt is defined as a response to an event in which someone else experienced loss but you did not." [31] I sometimes wonder why God still me has here and why others were called to glory. On many occasions I question if I'm doing enough to honor the lives of those whose paths I've crossed and are no longer here to live. Am I worthy to still be here and am I doing enough to prove my existence?

Angie

One of the most difficult things to face after surviving a traumatic life-threatening experience is losing those you care about to the very disease that tried to take your life.

It was a blistering cold day and I was still undergoing chemotherapy. My mom usually had a standing hair appointment at Willie His & Hers hair salon. Ms. Iona or Miss D. would pick her up and bring her home since at times I was too weak to drive. On this particular Wednesday I was asleep and was awakened to a familiar voice yelling,

"Hey, Nina!"

I sat up in my bed and knew that could only be one person, Wardene. As a little girl everyone in the neighborhood would call me by my middle name, Janeen, but those who really had a vested interest in my rearing called me "Nina." Wardene

---

[31] https://centerstone.org/our-resources/health-wellness/understanding-survivors-guilt/

was one of my first babysitters as a little girl and loved me like I was her family. She saw my mom at the hair salon and told her she would bring her home. Although I was embarrassed to see Wardene because my head was completely bald and the nausea had set in from the prior chemotherapy, seeing her brought me back to a time when I was little Nina - healthy, free and safe.

She began to tell me about her sister Angie who was fighting her own battle with cancer and encouraged me to call her because she would be able to help support me as someone who could identify with my journey. I called Angie and we talked, laughed, reminisced about growing up on Pennington Drive. She would continue to call and check on me until she couldn't any longer. Angie fought her battle with cancer until God called her home on May 29th, 2017. I traveled to her funeral in Maryland to say goodbye. I hope she knew how much I treasured her selflessness and love.

A few weeks later I was at work when I received a call from a man trying to take care of an account owned by his deceased wife. We began talking and he said Angie's full name. I told her husband who I was and that I made remarks at her funeral. He remembered me and we both cried. Out of over a thousand people he could have spoken to that day, God saw fit that he was connected to me. I was able to resolve his issue and give him peace of mind as he mourned.

"God knew what he needed that day" he said
And I agreed.

Cathy

The end of 2017 I received a call from my biological brother telling me my biological mother Cathy had cancer. I was not sure how to react as our relationship was strained and our conversation was almost nonexistent. I called her to let her know I was here; she acknowledged my call but I never heard from her after that day.

A Saturday in April 2018 my brother called again to tell me that Cathy was at Woodbury hospital in the ICU. I pulled into a CVS parking lot in shock unaware that she was that sick. I asked if it was okay for me to go see her and if she asked for me. The little girl in me wanted to believe that she asked for me and wanted to see me. He told me no but knew she would want me to be there. He expressed that I may not have another chance to see her otherwise.

After speaking with my brother, I went to the hospital to see Cathy. They told me my biological sister and Cathy's husband had just left. Have you ever cried without mummering a word? I did that day and I can't explain the dejection I felt seeing her that night. I felt a hand on my shoulder - it was the nurse. She asked me if I was her daughter and I said,

"Yes."

I held her hand and reminisced about the good times that we had shared and thanked her for hiding me in her belly for six months so that I could live. While I was there, another brother came and together, we sat with her in silence. I took a picture of my hand holding hers and sent it to my brother who told me she was in ICU. To this day I still have this picture. Cathy passed May 3rd, 2018, due to complications from cancer. I loved her and she will always be remembered.

Forgiveness is commanded, but reconciliation is conditional. I've learned that there are instances when we don't have a choice.

Monica

In 2013 or 2014 I was invited to a New Year's Eve prayer luncheon. There was a woman sitting at my table proudly talking about her daughter. She was telling us how much she loved her daughter and how ill she was with cancer. She repeatedly said that she wished she could take her illness from her. With tears in her eyes, she asked for prayer to remove the cancer from her daughter's body so that she could be there for her two sons.

As the women talked, I comforted her and asked her daughter's name.

"Monica." She shared.

I kindly asked her daughter's last name and she told me as well. It took me a moment but I made the connection. I immediately knew who her daughter was and had heard about her cancer journey. We both graduated from Rancocas Valley Regional High School in 1989 but were not friends. She had her friends and I had mine and there was never an ill word spoken between us however we just didn't connect in that way.

In 2017, Monica responded to a post about my cancer journey and triple negative breast cancer. We made plans to meet at her home and she mentioned Jenn, another classmate who had also fought cancer would be there too.

Monica, Jenn and I ate, talked, laughed, cried and reminisced until after midnight. I found out that night that Monica's mom had passed. I was in complete shock and all I could think about was the chance meeting I had with her mother that New Year's Eve and if Monica knew. I saw the pain in Monica's eyes as she talked about missing her and the undeniable love they shared. I was so thankful that I had the opportunity to tell Monica about the chance meeting with her mom at the House of Prayer in Westampton and the words her mom spoke about her.

I believe God placed me at the House of Prayer that day as a divine appointment for Monica and her mother. When her mother prayed for Monica, I felt God's presence and knew He would answer as only He could, not our will but His will be done. I will never forget this night, the night that ignited the beginning of our friendship.

A few months later I had a gathering at my home and invited Monica. She was hesitant but I asked her to trust me. I told her my home was a safe place and the afternoon would be easy and no stress. When she showed up, we hugged, teared up and I said,

"Girl I'm just working on this friendship."

"Janeen...we are friends." She replied.

On the morning of July 17th, 2019, I woke up with Monica on my mind. I called her but she did not answer. I did not find that strange because there were times she kept to herself. Later that afternoon I got the call that she had passed away.

Monica was a light and a fighter. We had several conversations I will never repeat and I will be forever loyal. Monica had many friends and family that loved her and although I only spent limited time with her our time was genuine and meaningful. I miss her and I will honor her memory by how I live.

If you don't believe God is real, I ask you to pay attention to how you are connected to others because there is always a purpose. I have attended more funerals than I care to say and grieved the loss of many I held close to my heart including my grandmother, grandfather, dear friends and friends that I considered family, however nothing prepared me for the loss to come.

Chapter 10
Her Name Was Agnes

"Fear not, for I am with you; be not dismayed, for I am your God; I will strengthen you, I will help you, I will uphold you with my righteous right hand." [32]

---

[32] *Isaiah 41:10 NKJV*

My first love was and will always be my mother, Adell Stevens. As a little girl I knew how blessed I was to call her mom. She became my foster mother at the age of 43 and adopted me when she was 45. To me, she was the most beautiful woman I had ever seen. Growing up she would work long hours as a nurse aid/assistant caring for the elderly patients. She would come home exhausted but still took excellent care of my brother and I.

Almost every night there was a warm meal and it was an event to order out on the weekends from Chicken Holiday or Sal's Pizza. She washed all our clothes, ironed and folded them until we moved out on our own. My mother showed love by her actions more so than through her words. I grew up in a home where "I love you" was not readily said but you knew you were loved. This was that old school type of love that today I understand.

My mother was born and grew up in South Carolina near Myrtle Beach. Her mother died when she was six years old after giving birth to twin babies, one girl and one boy. Soon after her mother passed, the twin girl passed also leaving my mother and her baby brother as orphans living with different family members that would find room for them to stay. My mother would often tell my brother and I that her reason for becoming a foster parent is because she wanted to prevent children from feeling what she felt as a child. After coming to New Jersey and meeting my father they both decided to begin their family. Not soon after they put in their application to become foster parents my brother who has different biological parents arrived. Six months later they received a call of a baby girl that was three days old needing a temporary placement and they accepted. After I ate them out of house and home, as my dad always said, they decided to keep me and make their home my forever home. My mom, dad, brother and I became a family and I am forever grateful and thankful. My parents were my divine appointments.

In 2005 while living in Philadelphia and working for Children's Aid Society, I asked my father if I could come back home and pay the taxes on the house while saving money for my house. He quickly said yes and began to redo the room I would be staying in. He was so excited that I was coming back home. I would later find out that he was sick with prostate cancer which also developed into lung cancer. I am not certain but I believe he knew he was sick. I truly believe that God brought me home to be there for my parents, to help my father and prepare him to go to glory.

The morning of September 20th, 2006 was the day my father gave me power of attorney over his medical needs. It was the day they were taking him to Samaritan Hospice located in the hospital. He did not want to sign the medical papers to go to hospice for fear of them taking the house he had paid for and most important he wanted to make sure my mom would be taken care of and not left alone. I promised my dad that I would always be there for my mother and it was okay to rest if he was tired. At 4:35 that very day, my father went to be with the Lord our God.

A short time after my father passed, my mother decided to sell her home and move into a one floor apartment. Although that was her decision, I could tell that she was not content. When I decided to purchase my home, I asked her how she felt about living with me.

Her eyes lit up as I began to discuss the home buying process with her, getting approved for a mortgage and the properties my realtor would take me to see. My mother had one request which was for me to purchase a home in an area close to our family church.

On May 16th, 2013, my mother got her wish and watched me sign paper after paper. I truly believe she was proud of me and that my father was pleased. I continued to fulfill my promise to my dad, Charlie Ray Stevens.

Having a cancer diagnosis almost two years to the day of moving into our new home was something I never would have predicted. The roles had changed, it was my turn to take care of my mother and at this point in her life she could not take care of me. As I previously mentioned, the cancer diagnosis brought stress and anxiety because it was not just about me. I wanted to ensure she would be cared for with the same excellence that she cared for me.

Outside of the divine appointments that God placed in my life, journaling, prayer and my faith helped me cope with the multitude of emotions that I was facing at that time. I would be remiss if I did not say that the confidence my mother had in my fight and her faith helped me beyond words and measure. I am so blessed and thankful to have had my mother see me overcome my cancer diagnosis.

Having my mother live with me afforded me the opportunity to make new memories with her and get to know her not only as a mother but a woman. One of the most astonishing things I learned about my mother was her name. One evening after work I came home and my mother did not seem like herself. I remember asking her,

"Mom, what is your name?"

She said with sternness in her voice,

"My name is Agnes."

I asked her, "Who is Agnes?"

She said, "Agnes is my name."

I believed for her to be in the early stages of dementia. I later found out my mom's name was not Adell, it was actually Agnes Adell. She never liked the name Agnes and chose to use her middle name Adell. I had lived 49 years and never knew my mother's name. This is just one of the fun, loving and quirky memories I have with and of my mother.

Even during covid I made sure to keep up with my mother's doctor appointment. To my knowledge my mom was healthy. At every appointment, her doctors would boast about her excellent blood work and health. They could not believe she could be 92 and truth be told she had better discipline than I when it came to her daily routine. Although at times she became forgetful and I saw signs of early dementia, she was just amazing in how she got around the house and functioned. My working from home due to covid gave her peace and comfort. She would often say how thankful she was that I was home and so was I.

During one of her doctor visits, her primary doctor and I discussed her getting a precautionary mammogram and a colonoscopy. You see, doctors rarely recommend a mammogram for anyone over the age of 75. Insurance companies generally don't want to cover the expense of this unless you ask for it or a doctor recommends it.

Her primary doctor gave me a referral and it was approved. Again, we did not expect to find anything. Remember, all her blood work was good and there were no signs of anything abnormal. Later that afternoon I received a call that my mother's tests found a small mass in her breast. I was shocked. I quickly had to make some decisions on her behalf. I made an appointment with a breast surgeon for later that week and decided to not tell my mother because I did not want her to worry. I told her the day prior that she had a follow up appointment just for preventative measure.

After the biopsy and meeting with the breast surgeon my mother was diagnosed with stage 2 breast cancer and we were told it was not aggressive. Due to her age the doctor recommended no surgery but instead for her to take a low dose oral chemotherapy medication.

There are two points I want to share to help anyone who has an aging parent or an elderly parent that has been newly diagnosed with breast cancer.

1) Be an advocate. I mentioned that after the age of 75 you must ask for a mammogram as it's not always recommended. Her doctor supported us in this decision but not every physician will approve or recommend a mammogram.

2) When you get a mammogram, it only scans your breast, but when you are diagnosed with breast cancer it's so important to also get a chest x-ray to identify if there is any cancer in the lung or chest.

As time progressed, I had concerns about her shortness of breath so I had a follow up appointment with her heart doctor. He checked her lungs and said everything seemed okay and my mother had a history of allergies which he believed was the cause of her shortness of breath. I asked for and was adamant about scheduling a chest x-ray and EKG. He was hesitant but scheduled it.

The following week my mother came home from her hair appointment and had extreme shortness of breath. She was recovering from a bad cold and had been tested for covid so I figured she may just need to rest. As I helped her inside, she kept telling me she was fine but a bit winded. I helped her in her chair and even though she said she was fine, I knew she was not herself. I called my employer to tell them I needed to sign off early because my mother was ill and I needed to get her to the emergency room.

When we got to the hospital everyone was telling her how good she looked, even her breathing was getting better. When the nurse called her back, I told my mother that I loved her and that she would be fine. Usually, I would never leave her side but due to covid regulations they would not let me go back with her. So I told her I would be waiting when they were done.

When the nurse told me she had pneumonia and they needed to keep her overnight, it made perfect sense. I thought, "of course, that must be the cause of her cough and shortness of breath." I asked the nurse to let me speak to her so that she could hear my voice before I left. I promised my mother that I would be back early the next morning to bring her home.

The next morning, I was preparing myself to go to the hospital when her doctor called to tell me that he needed to run more tests, however from his experience we learned my mother had stage 4 lung cancer. All I remember saying was,

"Don't tell my mother, I will be there in 20 minutes."

I fell to my knees and sat there in shock asking God to direct my steps. I immediately thought of my father and what he went through and asked God to not let this be true for my mother. I believe that God afforded me the ability to have gone through my diagnosis and heal to be able to now take care of my mother.

I reminisced of the day I had a gathering at my home to thank my divine appointment for being obedient and being a blessing in my life. I gave each of them a card with a butterfly on the front and inside was a message expressing my gratitude and love. I wrote inside my mother's card that I promised her that if there was time she forgot, I would remember and I would never leave her alone. She kept that card on her dresser because it meant something to her. With everything in me, I was going to keep my promise.

After getting a second opinion at MD Anderson I was told the cancer was indeed stage 4 lung cancer and there was nothing that could be done. I looked at my mother who knew her time was limited and promised her that I would never leave her and we were going to live until God wanted her home and that's what we did. I started asking her even more about her journey, fears, triumphs and love of God. She was so faithful and strong. I told her over and over how much I loved her and how proud I was of her. I am so proud to call her mom.

I remember the day I was told by hospice to begin giving her morphine. It was a Friday evening and I could tell her breathing was labored. The next day was the first time she had an appetite. A neighbor who is now a dear friend, Keva Marie, had brought us dinner that evening. I had no idea that would be the last meal my mother would eat. She told me she was tired and wanted me to prepare her for bed. As I laid her down, I kissed her and told her I loved her and she told me that she loved me. I asked her what I did almost every night for five years,

"Mom, do you feel comfortable? Do you feel safe? Do you feel loved?"

"Yes." She responded.

We also had a sleep tight joke. Every night I would say,

"Sleep tight don't let the bedbugs bite and she would say something like,

"It's too cold in here for some bed bugs or there better not be any bed bugs."

It bothers me that I can't remember what she said that particular night. I miss my mother so much.

That evening after putting my mom to bed I slept on the couch outside her room because I needed to be there and I was not going to leave her alone. I watched her sleep so peacefully as if she was not sick and in perfect peace.

When she woke up in the middle of the night I awoke to her sitting on the side of the bed because she had no strength in her legs to go to the bathroom. I ran to her bedside and lifted her in her wheelchair to get her into the bathroom. Even though I worked out and lifted weights at the gym It was hard for me to lift her. It took us 45 minutes to get her in the bathroom and back to bed. A few hours later we needed to repeat the same process and it was even more difficult. She cried and I told her it was okay and I didn't mind. I was strong and could do it.

A couple hours later she called for me, her voice slurred and needed me to take her again to the bathroom but she was even weaker and I couldn't lift her in the wheelchair. I kissed her cheek and told her it was okay for her to urinate in the depends I had put on her. I looked in her eyes and told her to try and I did not mind cleaning her. She looked at me with sadness in her eyes that I had never seen before. I told her I loved her and, in that moment, I knew she would be leaving me. It hurt her for me to have to do this for her, she was so independent.

As I laid my mother down it was hard to change her and I needed her changed, covered and comfortable. A neighbor, Denise, who was also a caregiver to her mother, came to help me. I think my call to her was,

"We need you."

And I burst in tears. Denise immediately came to help me. At all costs I needed my mom to feel safe, loved and comfortable. That morning I made the decision to have a urinary catheter placed for my mother. I wanted her to stay home. I promised to never leave her alone and I was going to keep my promise to my mother.

You never know why or how God puts certain people in your life until you are in the moment when all you can see is God and feel the strength that can only come from Him.

Four years prior I was invited to a fabulous event to support the Yvonne McCalla Foundation Incorporated, a nonprofit breast cancer awareness organization. Two beautiful women came up to me and introduced themselves, Karen and Lisa. Karen recognized me from a post we both commented on in support of a person we knew whose mother had Alzheimer's. I immediately connected with these two ladies. I did not know Karen was married to a man in ministry and the role she would play in my life for such a time as this.

My mom's health began to quickly decline and I began to decline mentally and physically. Everyone kept telling me how strong I was and all I could think about was how my heart was breaking. Seeing my strong mother so weak was more than I could bear but I knew I had to be strong for her. No one and nothing prepares you for helping your parents go to glory except for God's strength, mercy and the divine appointments He puts in place. During my mom's decline, Karen came by and stayed for over twelve hours. She sat with my mom and rubbed her hand, prayed over her with such love and care. There were some words I could hear her speak to my mothers and others were mere sounds. As I watched in the distance, I understood why God connected Karen and I - it was the love we shared for our mothers.

During this time so many would come to see my mom to love on her, pray for her, my brother and I. It is my belief that she heard every prayer spoken over her including the private prayer I spoke as I held her in the midnight hour when she woke up in distress. The last week of her life I would sleep on the floor holding her hand because I know she was scared of being alone.

As a little girl I would always pray for God to keep my mom alive until I was 50. I thought that that was old and since my mother was older when she adopted me, that was the proper request and would not be asking too much. Well, God honored my prayer.

Wednesday, September 22nd, 2021, at 1:45 pm my mother took her last breath. I had briefly stepped out and my brother was with her. I called home to tell my brother I was around the corner and he told me she was asleep. As soon as I hung up less than a minute later, he called to tell me she was gone. When I walked in the room I called hospice, held her as her spirit left her body, the same as I did for my dad. I felt a breeze come through the crack of the window. I believe that was her going to be with the Lord.

As the hospice nurse and social worker came to prepare my mom for the funeral home, I began to wash my mother's feet, lotion them and put matching blue fuzzy socks on her to match the blue nightgown and robe she had changed into; blue was her favorite color. I kissed her and checked on my brother - his wife had arrived to be with him. Thinking of her being wheeled out of our home into the hearse and watching her leave hurts like the day it happened. She passed almost 15 years to the day my dad passed.

My brother and his wife would not leave until someone came to be with me. I looked up and Karen was coming in the door. I called Cindy, and she said she would be here within the hour as she was coming from her home in Philadelphia. The neighbors that are today my friends came immediately to support me. I am forever grateful for everyone present that evening, prior and after as their love and support came to me as divine appointments.

Two weeks before my mother passed, I played the songs for her that would be played at her funeral, songs that crossed my mind as I knew this day would one day come. The songs played at her funeral were the songs she agreed to be sung. I asked her what color she wanted to be buried in and the color of the casket that she requested. Dena would not take no for an answer and came with me to pick out her casket. I am forever grateful.

Denise and I had noticed the jacket to my mom's suit needed to be fastened because she was pristine in her appearance and would not want the jacket open at the top. While my mom laid in her room asleep, Denise took her suit jacket home to sew the hook and eye on the top of her jacket to keep it closed. My heart is still full.

Having that conversation with my mother was the most difficult conversation I ever had in my life outside of telling my dad that it was okay to go to glory and rest. Cindy packed clothes for several days, as she did when my father passed, my first surgery and now to support and help me as I prepared for my mother's burial. I could not write the obituary or program because it was so final to me. We wrote her obituary and program close to midnight a few days before the funeral. She knows me almost better than I know myself. She was exhausted but knew I knew I needed to be ready. God, I thank you for my sister, Cindy! I always tell her not everyone has a Cindy and I thank God; He loved me enough to give me an older sister over twenty years ago.

My mother's funeral was beautiful and I hope she was proud. Karen graciously spoke at my mother's funeral on my behalf because I did not have the strength to speak for myself. Her words conveyed everything I could not and in such a way that undeniably honored my mother. I'm forever grateful!

I had lost members of my family, my father, biological mother, grandmother, grandfather, close friends and now my mother. For many difficult life events and funerals my dear sister/friend Carita has been present. When I did not have the emotional strength and I could not be present she encouraged me and reminded me who and Whose I was. Carita is a phenomenal speaker and graciously took time to prepare a remembrance for both of my parents and she spoke at their funerals. She had just lost her mother a year ago and saw fit to be there for me. There are no words to thank her for helping to send both my parents' home.

My God gave me a mother who knew the importance of feeling wanted, safe, comfortable and loved because there were times in her life she did not feel this for herself. Even at the age of 92, she still felt hurt from her childhood trauma. While I believe my mother was my divine appointment, I know I was hers as well. Together we did a thing by showing the world that love is love and family can be created out of this love.

It was not easy for my mother to take care of me nor was it easy for me to be there for her but God saw fit to place us in each other's lives because he knew what we needed on our journey. My mother, Adell Stevens, will always be my most treasured divine appointment and the reason I started to believe that I could actually not only encourage myself but others to live.

Chapter 11

...And What If You Live?

"For I know the plans I have for you, declares the Lord, plans for welfare and not for evil, to give you a future and a hope."[33]

---

[33] *Jerimiah 29:11 ESV*

And what if you live without fear, anxiety, depression nor regret, but with God's promises for your life? What if you live accepting what God says about you and receiving His word as truth and boldly walking into your purpose? And What if you live?

It was quiet, in fact it was too quiet for me. The phone had stopped ringing and all I had was time to walk around our home that was fashioned with my mother in mind. Everything reminded me of her and I missed her more than words could express. On this particular day, I went to the mailbox and I was surprised to receive a card from my mother's doctor that read,

"From what I can see you've taken excellent care of your mother. Your mom is at peace, I sure hope that you are."

Although I felt I did the best I could, I still grieved the loss of my mother and I was not at peace. When you are caregiving, you think about the time you will have when it's just you but if I am truthfully honest, time means nothing when your purpose and your loved one is no longer with you. I had willingly devoted so much time to my mother's wellbeing that I felt an enormous emptiness and void without her. I had lost my identity and truth be told I felt like an orphan. Yet again, I was forced to adapt to another new normal that I was not ready to accept.

Almost one week to the day I buried my mother my friend Carie called me. She said,

"I know you are mourning but I have time this week to help you get things in order in regard to your mother's room."

Carie and I had talked about her helping me after the funeral, however it had only been a week. If anyone knows beautiful Carie, you know her heart is gold and she means well. Carie had experienced a lot of loss and hurt so her response to help me take the next step came with no surprise but with gratitude.

I asked Carie to give me a day or so to find an organization to accept my mother's beloved suits and hats that she wore to church. I wanted to make sure her clothes would be donated to a place that she would approve. After placing my call to the local nonprofit, within an hour I received a call from Patricia. I had not heard her voice since I was a teenager.

She began to give her condolences for the loss of my mom and to tell me that she was Development Director for this nonprofit and when she was told about my call that she knew it was me. Speaking to Pat brought such peace to my decision and enabled me to begin the process of taking the first step in preparing some of her items to be donated. Pat was my divine appointment.

Prior to Carrie's arrival, I decided to remove the purse my mother was using so that it would not get mixed in with the donated items. As I looked through her purse and wallet, she had only a few pictures, one of my fathers, my brother in middle school and one of me in the first grade. I noticed a business card that looked familiar. It was a business card that I had given her a year prior when I was telling her I wanted to start a nonprofit named …And What If You Live? I explained to her that its mission would be to help and encourage others who were navigating through a diagnosis or life challenge to live. Seeing the business card brought tears to my eyes because I knew it meant something to her. She was listening to me, saw me and believed in me.

I began to reminisce of when I first designed the business card and received the vision for And What If You Live. In 2020, one year prior to my mother's passing, a dear friend Pam who I had met while working at a non-profit in Camden, NJ asked me to join her for a weekly bible study. It was at the height of covid and the fellowship was needed. The group started as Pam, Natalie, Valerie, Zondra and me. We studied God's word and encouraged each other to achieve God's purpose for our life. While doing a book study on Marshawn Evans Daniels Book, Dream Bigger, God's calling for my life became even more clear and evident. Not only did our group provide support to discover our purpose but it would provide encouragement as we individually dealt with loss, grief and a cancer diagnosis.

God connected us for a time such as this and we became each other's divine appointments. Four of us still meet bimonthly to assist, support and encourage each other while studying God's word. Weeks following my mother's passing, I received a call from Cindy who said to me that God spoke to her and said that I needed to move forward with And What If You Live because there were people in the waiting room.

I received confirmation from God, my mother and big sister but grief and fear were still holding me back. I saw a recent interview from TD Jake's that resonated with me. He said,

"Redefine your life and do not try to reduplicate what was because it will never be again. Whether it's through death, aging or sickness you don't get to do a redo, so reset and figure out what makes you happy. Figure out what makes you happy and have the power to create your own moment rather than become a target for misery." [34]

I began to look for a therapist because I knew I needed to heal in order to move forward. During covid it was nearly impossible to find a therapist. I remember googling a therapist in the area and came across the name of psychiatrist, Dr. Bryana Carrea. It was after 7pm on a Tuesday evening and I felt led to call her. To my surprise her assistant answered the phone. My appointment was scheduled under the premise that I was a current client of hers. I believe this was God's plan.

When I arrived at her office that following Tuesday, I was surprised to see bible scripture and words of encouragement on the walls and the feeling of peace and respite upon entering her office. Not only was Dr. Carrea a licensed psychiatrist but also a Christian and a steadfast believer in God's word. I knew I

---

[34] *Bishop T.D. Jakes*

was in the right place when she prayed with me before and after my initial session. Dr. Carrea is a divine appointment that I thank God for every day. She has and continues to bless me beyond measure. I now was ready to say "yes" and walk in my purpose. God had set me free.

61 1-7 " The Spirit of God, the Master, is on me
  because God anointed me.
He sent me to preach good news to the poor,
  heal the heartbroken,
Announce freedom to all captives,
  pardon all prisoners.
God sent me to announce the year of his grace—
  a celebration of God's destruction of our enemies—
  and to comfort all who mourn,
To care for the needs of all who mourn in Zion,
  give them bouquets of roses instead of ashes,
Messages of joy instead of news of doom,
  a praising heart instead of a languid spirit.
Rename them "Oaks of Righteousness"
  planted by God to display his glory.
They'll rebuild the old ruins,
  raise a new city out of the wreckage.
They'll start over on the ruined cities,
  take the rubble left behind and make it new.

You'll hire outsiders to herd your flock" [35]
and foreigners to work your fields,
But you'll have the title "Priests of God,"
honored as ministers of our God.
You'll feast on the bounty of nations,
you'll bask in their glory.
Because you got a double dose of trouble
and more than your share of contempt,
Your inheritance in the land will be doubled
and your joy go on forever.
8-9 "Because I, God, love fair dealing
and hate thievery and crime,
I'll pay your wages on time and in full,
and establish my eternal covenant with you.
Your descendants will become well-known all over.
Your children in foreign countries
Will be recognized at once
as the people I have blessed."
10-11 I will sing for joy in God,
explode in praise from deep in my soul!
He dressed me up in a suit of salvation,
he outfitted me in a robe of righteousness,
As a bridegroom who puts on a tuxedo
and a bride with a jeweled tiara.
For as the earth bursts with spring wildflowers,

---

[35] *"Announce Freedom of All Captives" Isaiah 61: 1-11 MSG*

and as a garden cascades with blossoms,
So the Master, God, brings righteousness into full bloom
and puts praise on display before the nations.

I was previously certified as a life coach and I had already begun seeing clients. I start every initial session with asking my clients if they felt comfortable, safe and loved. These are the same questions I asked my mother every night before bed. I've named this Adell's Assessment. This has proven to be a great starting point for my clients and establishes trust.

Within a year God would allow me to finalize the trademark; start the process of the LLC for the life coaching under my name, have a website created, form a board of directors and have ...*And What If You Live?* approved for a 501(C)3 to assist those seeking to move forward from a diagnosis and life change to discover new direction, create new purpose, and live more aligned with their values. Also, a Facebook page, *"...And What If You Live?"* was launched to provide daily encouragement and support to encourage others to truly live.

It is my wish and desire for And What If You Live to be known as a MOVEMENT that partners with individuals and organizations to provide resources, financial support and in-kind donations to those who have experienced a cancer diagnosis. Our driving force is to give hope, encouragement, motivation and inspiration to live.

To honor my mother, the Adell's Angels Fund was established to assist those directly providing in-home care to a loved one who has been diagnosed with cancer.

As so many, I fight for my life every day and seek God to light my path. I've chosen to believe in God's promises for my life. I stand firm and intentional when asking for His support, guidance and strength. There were days I could not "move" and have been paralyzed due to not only mental and physical exhaustion but fear of the unknown. I often say to my friends that I don't know much about King James or James King but I do know this, God only asked me for one thing and that was for me to accept His Son Jesus Christ as my personal Savior and He would give me eternal life. Because of this I have chosen to not walk in fear but in his divine purpose for my life. When your belief meets actual purpose - you become unstoppable

My faith allowed me to meet God's divine appointments and have clarity to recognize each of them even through seasons of illness, grief, sadness and depression. At every opportunity He showed me that He is God and that He never left me. He did this for me and He can do the same for you.

I have one question ...And What If You Live?

40 Days of Reflection and Encouragement
...And What If You Live?

"All it takes is one moment. God can flip it, turn it, release it, remix it, reverse it, approve it, do it, grant it, remove it, increase it - in one moment." [36]

It is my hope that despite grief, loss, a life disappointment, diagnosis or challenge you are able to reflect on God's love and promises for your life. To know He is the same God and will never leave or forsake you. By believing in Him all things can be made possible and your day anew.

Day 1

When I look over my life, I see a God that Has worked miracles and has carried me through life disappointments. Although I know God's hand is on my life, if I am honest, there are moments of disappointment because of deferred dreams, life challenges and grief.

As I began to focus on my relationship with God, being honest with Him about my feelings, and repeating His promises to me a shift began in my daily life...it was then I wanted to "live," truly live in expectation of what God has for me. It was then I was okay with my "today."

---

[36] RealTalkKim

I've learned that it is important to stop thinking what it should be like, God will show us what it will be like. Selfcare is trusting God's promises.

Your life will change when you learn to depend on the promises of God.

"For I know the plans I have for you, declares the Lord, plans for welfare and not for evil, to give you a future and a hope."[37]

What are you believing in God for today?

Day 2

I remember speaking with someone I love dearly and she began to tell me that she felt alone. She would go on to tell me that she felt as if she was there for everyone but no one was there for her. You see, she had dreams but she felt she had no midwives to help her birth what God had put on her heart to do. As I listened to her talk for several minutes uninterrupted, I asked her one question,

"Is this true?"

You see what my sister/friend felt were her feelings and her feelings were valid but did she truly have no one that "saw her," "cared for her," "sewed into her," believed in her," "would fight with her for her wins," and would pray with her or for her when she couldn't?"

---

[37] *Jeremiah 29:11 ESV*

Although there are days, she may still have some of these thoughts, I hope and pray she never forgets our conversation.

If you feel alone, please know God wants to give us peace for loneliness and rest from overwhelming sadness. God asks us to take our burdens to Him. Mathew 11: 28-30.

For me he has answered my prayers in so many miraculous ways including my divine appointments. I know and believe He will do the same for you.

Self-care is knowing when to ask yourself, "is this true?" Self-care is being ok saying God; I need you to show me Your truth because on my own it's just not adding up and I can't see the forest because of the trees. It's ok to tell God with expectation for an answered prayer.

"Don't let your hearts be troubled. Trust in God, and trust in me." [38]

What untruths are you telling yourself?

<u>Day 3</u>

Give yourself grace, remember the things you can control and give everything else to God. Things you can control: Your attitude, your effort, how well you plan, how well you love people, how hard you work, your consistency, your faithfulness,

---

[38] *John 14:1 NLT*

how you take care of yourself, how kind you are to others, your prayers, how you show up, how you chose to try again after a failure.

"Let us then with confidence draw near to the throne of grace, that we may receive mercy and find grace to help in time of need." [39]

What are you giving up to God?

<u>Day 4</u>

"One day you will find someone that chooses you and continues to choose your everyday, and that's when you will be happy things happened the way they did." - Author Unknown

Fourteen years ago, I was sitting in Church and a few rows ahead of me I saw the cutest little girl staring at me while looking over her mother's shoulder. She would look at me, smile and during the time set for fellowship, she would dash off following me wherever I went. This 3-year-old little girl would later ask to sit with me. She would sit on my lap and fall asleep and look so peaceful. Her mother noticed our connection and our bond. She asked me to be her daughter's godmother and I accepted.

This little girl, now seventeen-year-old teenager is and has been a consistent blessing in my life. She is wise beyond her

---

[39] *Hebrews 4:16 ESV*

years and loves me by her actions, heart and words. She chooses me and for this my heart stays full.

Self-care is accepting and making time for those who "choose you," see you and love you without condition. The ones that light up when they see you, hear your voice and only want your time. Me giving my time replenishes me and gives life back to my soul. I'm so thankful I said yes 14 years ago and became a godmother to my Nayomi.

"Commit your work to the Lord, and your plans will be established." [40]

Is there anyone that you need to make time for that has been waiting on you? Is that person you?

<u>Day 5</u>

Last week I had some errands to run on my lunch break and as I was leaving the house, I realized that I did not have my phone. I began to quickly look everywhere for the phone but could not find it. As I kept revisiting where I might have left it, in frustration I asked God to please help me. It was at that moment I heard my phone ring...my phone was in the refrigerator.

---

[40] *Proverbs 16:3 AMP*

I saw a recent post that reminded me:

If God cares about me finding my phone, He certainly cares about major things, such as what I desire for my life.

TRUST THAT GOD WILL MEET YOUR NEEDS TODAY.

Do not go by for a second without knowing that God sees you and He cares about every detail of your life.

Even when God doesn't answer prayers in the ways we expect, we can trust that He supplies both our wants and needs according to his perfect plan. We serve a God that is a provider.

You don't have to worry. Bring every need to Him, bring every request to Him.

This reminder blessed me and I hope it blesses you as well. Self-care is giving it All to God and trusting He cares for your every need.

"Do not be anxious about anything, but in everything by prayer and supplication with thanksgiving let your requests be made known to God." [41]

"I can do all things through him who strengthens me." [42]
Philippians 4:13

What are you trusting God for today?

---

[41] *Philippians 4:6 ESV*
[42] *Philippians 4:13 ESV*

<u>Day 6</u>

As my mother got older naturally she would move slower. On any given Sunday morning I would hear her stirring around in her room preparing for church service. I knew her routine because she was consistent and prepared for the day. There were days she did not want to get up and wanted to rest but she prayed, pushed through and when arriving at her destination God made sure she had the support she needed.

Whatever you are going through today I encourage you to keep going, encourage yourself, pray and push through. Ask God to give you the strength you need and to have support in place. He loves you and will never leave your side. Ask me how I know?

"Seek the Lord and his strength; seek his presence continually.[43]

In what areas are you asking for strength and perseverance?

<u>Day 7</u>

Has there ever been a time when you were going through a season of illness, hurt, pain, rejection or despair and there was nothing no one could provide to give you comfort or peace? My answer is yes.

---

[43] *1 Chronicles 16:11 ESV*

I remember finding out that I would not be able to have children. Being adopted I always wanted a child that looked like me. To everyone It seemed as if I were ok, but only God knew the true desires of my heart. I took my broken heart and all its pieces to Him in prayer and He answered in the most unexpected way. Today I am so blessed and thankful to have a daughter that loves me so and I love with all my heart.

Whatever you are going through, go to God in prayer...prayer is the best self-care. It can bring alignment with God. It can elicit feelings of gratitude, compassion, and forgiveness; all of which are associated with healing and hope.

Prayer is the best self-care. Netflix, coffee, nature, books, quality time with quality friends-these are great sources of comfort. Yet nothing beats the refreshing power of spending time in honest prayer.

"Praying at all times in the Spirit, with all prayer and supplication. To that end, keep alert with all perseverance, making supplication for all the saints," [44]

What season are you praying for today?

---

[44] *Ephesians 6:18 NLT*

<u>Day 8</u>

Every day is not easy but is it supposed to be? There are going to be occasions when we are called to do things outside of our comfort zone, that will give God glory and demonstrate His goodness and mercy. I encourage you to trust God, His discernment and promises for your life ...challenge anything within your thoughts stopping you from "moving" for His glory.

Have a great day making new memories! Don't Limit your challenges, challenge your limits.

"Do not be conformed to this world, but be transformed by the renewal of your mind, that by testing you may discern what is the will of God, what is good and acceptable and perfect." [45] *Romans 12:2*

What is challenging your thoughts and stopping you from moving forward?

<u>Day 9</u>

There are times I finagle my day to have everything exact, scheduled and tasked completed but there are also days when I completely miss the mark.

I've learned that our to-do's and our journey will not be perfect but we must take active steps towards our growth, focus

---

[45] *Romans 12:2*

on what serves us well, give ourselves grace and know that we can do all things through Christ Jesus.

I had a day full of to-do's today... but a special young lady called and said, "Mom, I'm coming to see you today." My small voice told me what was important.

Train yourself to listen to that small voice that tells us what's important and what's not.

"But if it is by grace, it is no longer on the basis of works; otherwise, grace would no longer be grace." [46]

What are you giving yourself grace for today?

Day 10

May you witness God's promises of beauty for ashes today.

Beauty for ashes He brought me,

Sweet oil of joy for my tears

Anthems of praise He has taught me,

To replace the pain of my years.

Comfort He brings to the broken,

The Healer of grief-stricken hearts;

By blessed words He has spoken,

Love, joy, and peace He imparts.

---

[46] *Romans 11:16 KJV*

High Hope is He to the hopeless,

While souls bound by sin He set free;

A shelter of rest for the homeless,

A Help to the helpless is He.

Healing He brings to the ailing,

Yet, even at death's final hour,

He promises life never failing,

For He is the Source of All Power.

Whom is my simple song singing?

This One Who gives beauty for shame?

Messiah, to Whom I am clinging.

Christ Jesus, The Lord, is His Name!

-L.B. Chiaro

"To grant to those who mourn in Zion— to give them a beautiful headdress instead of ashes, the oil of gladness instead of mourning, the garment of praise instead of a faint spirit; that they may be called oaks of righteousness, the planting of the Lord, that he may be glorified."[47] Isaiah 61:3

What ashes are you giving to God in exchange for beauty?

---

[47] *Isaiah 61:3 NASB*

<u>Day 11</u>

You are enough and you are worthy. Y(
be perfect to fulfill the gifts God has put insidf

Everything you want to accomplish is already w₁ͳ
so when you start to roll in self-doubt and think negative
thoughts then you will fall off track and become distracted. So,
keep visualizing and knowing what you are destined for, it'll
come to you.

*"Worthy are you, our Lord and God, to receive glory
and honor and power, for you created all things, and by your
will they existed and were created."* [48]

What are visualizing for your life and future?

<u>Day 12</u>

He is with you! You are too precious to Him to have you
walk this journey alone. If you are lonely, hurt, anxious,
confused, whatever your need just invite God into your
situation.

God never lets you face a situation alone. He goes
before you. He stands with you. Whatever situation you're in,
be confident that God is always with you always.

---

[48] *Revelation 4:11 NIV*

"So don't worry, because I am with you. Don't be afraid, because I Am your God. I Will make you strong and will help you; I will support you with my right hand and save you" [49]
Isaiah 41:10

What situation are you inviting God into today?

Day 13

As we look at the busy day ahead be reminded of this quote.

"If you change the way you look at things, the things you look at change."

Today I chose to say, "I get to" rather than "I have to." Find a piece of joy in your day...it's there but we just need to see and receive it.

"Giving thanks always and for everything to God the Father in the name of our Lord Jesus Christ." Ephesians 5:20

Describe what you are grateful for today?

Day 14

The thing you could be praying for could be to simply get up and put one foot in front of the other, love you, see your

---

[49] *Isaiah 41:10 NASB*

worth and know that your life matters. Whatever this is for you...just know every step you take will lead to what God has for you.

It's worth the wait. That thing you're praying for is worth every tear and fiery trial. You're fighting for something beautiful, and it will soon be yours. God gave you a wonderful glimpse, but it won't compare to the final product. It's so much more than you know, child of God! Every promise is exceeding and abundant.

"Trust in the Lord with all your heart, and do not lean on your own understanding. In all your ways acknowledge him, and he will make straight your paths" [50]

What steps will you take to show God that you are willing to trust His promises for your future?

Day 15

"When we say yes to God's truth, we shed everything the world tells us we must do to prove ourselves."

Take the pressure off of you. You have nothing to prove to anyone. God has already said who you are to Him and that alone means you are enough.

---

[50] *Proverbs 3:5-6 ESV*

Self-care is knowing and believing with every fiber of your being that you are loved, worthy and valuable, made new and full of the Spirit, you are transforming, you are His child and His witness. He made no mistake when it came to creating you. With every breath you have purpose...this is God's truth about you. I'm believing in God...are you?

"I am the head and not the tail, and I only go upland not down in life as I trust and obey God." [51]

Do you feel as if you are enough? Do you see yourself the way God sees you? If not, why?

Day 16

Self-worth is self-care. Not one drop of yourself worth should depend on man's acceptance of you.

There were times in my life that I would wait for others to include me, value me, or show favor toward me before I would see myself as being worthy. Today I know I am enough based on the experiences God has brought me through, His word and who He says I am. Seek God's "yes."

May we always be aware of our self-worth and value, and act accordingly-to the honor and glory of God. "God, I praise you because I am fearfully and wonderfully made."

---

[51] *Deuteronomy 28:13* **AMPC**

"You alone are enough; you have nothing to prove to anyone."[52] - Maya Angelou

"For you formed my inward parts; you knitted me together in my mother's womb." [53]

What affects your self-worth?

<u>Day 17</u>

Self-care is sometimes saying "yes."

God put something in my spirit to birth at a time I wanted rest. I fought at every turn to say it was not the time and He became clear on the purpose He has for my life...He said it is the time.

I've always told people I am not a public speaker. I'm fine telling my testimony however at times it can be too heavy and takes me to a place of remembrance, trauma and fear. This is my truth. I fought through that fear and recently spoke as a keynote speaker, telling my breast cancer journey. My goal was to encourage others and give God the glory.

Self-care can mean saying yes to the hard things. Giving my testimony not only spoke to those present but also to my continued healing of what was, what is and what's to come. God is the same God and trusting Him and His plans gives peace in

---

[52] *Maya Angelou*
[53] *Psalms 139: 13-14*

the midst of noise and distraction. He wants us to have faith in His plans for us.

"For God did not give us the spirit of fear, but of power, love and of a sound mind" [54]

What are you saying "yes" to today?

<u>Day 18</u>

My truth? I know there is nothing I have been through, dealt with or have overcome that has been by my own doing.

Although your journey may be difficult you can overcome everything that was meant to stop you from "living." I encourage you to be intentional with your thoughts and to stand firm in your foundation.

Ask me how I know? I fight every day.

If Jesus is your foundation, you'll be able to withstand the storm.

"Open my eyes, that I may behold wondrous things out of your law." [55]

What storm are you withstanding?

<u>Day 19</u>

---

[54] *2 Timothy 1:7 NLT*
[55] *Psalm 119:18 NKJV*

This past week I was having an exceptional morning. The sun was out, the weather was amazing and I was able to get to the grocery store early...I was winning.

At the grocery store I saw an elderly woman trying to get an item off the shelf. As I tried to help her, she rudely said, "I don't need your help." At the checkout counter I was behind her...she looked at me and immediately turned away. As I walked out the store, she was waiting for me (I'm thinking...Is she determined to change the trajectory of my morning)? She began to apologize to me and with tears in her eyes she told me that she recently lost her daughter and that she was just diagnosed with stage 4 lung cancer. We cried, hugged, talked, and truly saw each other in that moment. A divine connection.

Self-care is being able to separate and not accept the energy from others that is not meant for you and not yours to carry. Her anger was not directed at me but to the pain in her heart.

There are so many that are hurting and are experiencing unimaginable pain due to a diagnosis, life disappointment and/or loss. It is important to understand that "grace" is for everyone.

You can't control how other people receive your energy. Anything you do or say gets filtered through the lens of whatever they are going through at the moment, which is not about you. Just keep doing "you" with as much integrity and love as possible.

"If any of you lacks wisdom, let him ask God, who gives generously to all without reproach, and it will be given to him."[56]

What are you releasing that is not yours to carry?

<u>Day 20</u>

There have been countless times in my life when I have tried to "fix" a person, situation or understand someone's rationale for the decisions they made that directly affected my heart.

Today my peace comes from knowing...truly knowing God is in control and He will carry all that burdens me.

All God asks is for us to lay our burdens down, bring "all" to Him and "trust" and "believe" He is God.

A part of my self-care is making a conscious decision to determine what I can control and what I cannot...if it's out of my control I give it to God.

"God is telling you today to be still. Stop stressing yourself over what is going on. Stop figuring it out with your own understanding. Stop fighting for it...because it's "Yours" already. God is saying, leave that to me to handle.

---

[56] *James 1:5*

"Be still, and know that I am God. I will be exalted among the nations, I will be exalted in the earth!" [57]

What are you trying to control that should be given to God?

Day 21

    You are here not by chance but by God's choosing to fulfill His purpose for this generation.

    God knows what He is doing. Don't be stressed. His timing is perfect. He has you right where He needs you to be...rest in His promises to you.

"When the Spirit of truth comes, he will guide you into all the truth, for he will not speak on his own authority, but whatever he hears he will speak, and he will declare to you the things that are to come." [58]

What purpose has God put on your heart to fulfill?

Day 22

    We want to change our circumstances, but God wants to use our circumstances to change us.

    There have been times in my life when I would go through the same situation over and over again and the outcome

---

[57] *Psalms 46:10 ESV*
[58] *John 16:13 ESV*

would remain the same. The day I realized that there was something I needed to love, learn, remove, make peace with, change, forgive or give grace to...I began to "live." It's never about the situation, it's about us, the changes we allow God to make within us and the plans He has for each of us.

"Create in me a clean heart, O God, and renew a right spirit within me." [59]

What changes do you need to make?

Day 23

I've recently decided to designate a closet in my home for prayer. It has been said that having a designated place to pray such as a prayer closet can eliminate stress and you can set yourself apart from everything around you.

I list my prayers for others, myself, prayers fulfilled, and affirmations of who God says I am; for me this helps with consistency and focus.

My bench and prayer pillow came last week. My prayer pillow is the artwork of a dear divine appointment and I love it and all that it represents!

Having a designated place to spend time with God is myself care. I take Him everywhere but my prayer closet is where I lay my and others burdens down. It is my safe place.

---

[59] *Psalms 51:10 KJV*

"But when you pray, go into your room and shut the door and pray to your Father who is in secret. And your father who sees in secret will reward you." [60]

Describe the place you love to spend time with God in prayer? Does it help with consistency and focus?

<u>Day 24</u>

Whatever you are going through know that there is no need to be afraid because God is in control. You only need to have faith in God knowing He will fight your battles until the very end. Today give all your worries to God and "live."

"The lord will fight for you; you need only be still." [61]

What anxieties, fears and doubts will you give to God today? What battle do you need God to fight on your behalf?

<u>Day 25</u>

The promises and blessings of God are not automatically fulfilled in our lives, they need to be activated by faith, prayer and works of faith. To activate God's promises in our life, we

---

[60] *Matthew 6:6 ESV*
[61] *Exodus 14:14 ESV*

need to be fully convinced that His word is true and what He has promised is His will for our life.

It is also important to know that God's promises are activated by what we SAY to Him, what comes out of our mouth. God honors the words that we say.

When God is invited, trusted and welcomed to move in your life...you ARE indeed living.

"So also faith by itself, if it does not have works, is dead."[62]

Describe your works of faith. Are you speaking the proper words over your life? Are you consistent in your actions?

Day 26

The enemy will tell you that when you go through a storm it's the judgment of God.

The truth of God's word? If He allows you to be in a storm it's by divine instruction.

God intends for us to see/receive something in that storm.

---

[62] *James 2:11 ESV*

God is not trying to destroy us- He wants to show us who He is on another dimension and level...He wants us to show our faith and trust Him.

Self-care is releasing the burden of carrying every concern, disappointment, fear, rejection, negative report on our own and trusting God is:

God Almighty

King of Kings

Jehovah Jireh

Jehovah Nissi

"Most High"

He is the same God and has the best intentions for us...He loves us.

"Peace I leave with you; my peace I give to you. Not as the world gives do I give to you. Let not your hearts be troubled, neither let them be afraid." [63]

What message are you receiving from your storm?

Day 27

When I look at her there are things I see that I love, things I want to work on to be the best version of myself and

---

[63] *John 14:27 NIV*

things I have no control over...but most importantly I see "me." It's important to spend honest time with yourself to understand your triggers when it comes to self-talk which is key to self-care.

We all talk to ourselves but it's how we speak to ourselves that truly matters. It's important to love all of you. Ask me how I know?

"Do not confess that negative thought in your mind, rather speak life to every situation around you." [64] *Proverbs 30:32*

You are strong

You are amazing

You are loved

You are not alone

You are tough

You are courageous

You are a fighter

"Death and life are in the power of the tongue." [65]

What is the origin of your negative self-talk? And what changes will you make to speak life over your day?

Day 28

---

[64] *Provers 30:32*
[65] *Proverbs 18:21 KJV*

I am still trying to navigate the Holidays while managing grief.

My truth? I miss my parents. During the Holiday's, the feeling of loneliness and sadness can seem even more prominent when experiencing the loss of a parent or loved one. Ask me how I know? However, I encourage you to add gratitude to your thoughts as you remember and reflect on your loved ones who have gone to glory.

I've found myself in the neighborhood I grew up in and eventually in front of my childhood home. I've cried with sadness of missing what was while praising God for cherished memories and what is to come.

I've learned that gratitude is a conscious daily practice and to conquer these seasons I must be intentional.

Selfcare is allowing yourself to reflect and remember with gratitude.

"The Lord is near the brokenhearted and saves the crushed in spirit." [66]

What memories are you grateful for?

Day 29

---

[66] *Psalms 34:18 ESV*

The first and last time my mother ever left the United States was to visit the Bahamas. I promised to show her water she could see through.

I recently took a much-needed vacation to the Bahamas, which was an emotional trip as I often thought of my mother and the memories we made on our trip.

A part of my self-care today is remembering the wonderful memories and allowing myself to shed tears for all that was and appreciating the opportunity we had to share a love like ours...perfectly imperfect, quirky and true.

Today I know it's ok to grieve your loved one...and while grieving to remember grief comes with beautiful memories that were made and tears are a part of the process.

"Blessed are those who mourn, for they shall be comforted." [67]

What are some of the fondest memories of your loved one? Have you allowed yourself to mourn and release so that you can live?

Day 30

"You have been assigned this mountain to show others it can be moved."

He is the same God that heard your cry in the midnight hour, gave you the energy to face another day and removed

---

[67] *Matthew 5:4 KJV*

obstacles that were meant to destroy you. Trust God and who He says He is in you and walk in that confidence.

"The Lord is my rock and my fortress and my deliverer, my God, my rock, in whom I take refuge, my shield, and the horn of my salvation, my stronghold." [68]

What mountains has God moved on your behalf that is evidence to you that He is the same God?

Day 31

"If I'd have done all the things I was supposed to have done, I'd be really tired." [69] - Willie Nelson

When you are looking at your life and all the "should have," "could have," and "would have," remember what "you have" accomplished despite everything that was meant to stop you. Remember to count it all!

"And we know that for those who love God all things work together for good, for those who are called according to his purpose." [70]

What have you accomplished despite what was meant to stop you?

<hr>

[68] *Psalms 18:2 KJV*
[69] *Willie Nelson*
[70] *Romans 8:28 ESV*

<u>Day 32</u>

I had no idea that I had a total of 10 brothers and sisters until May 10th, 1990. I never knew how you could love someone you never met until I met each of my siblings.

There was a time I felt guilty because I was not in their life, and after meeting them, I was 19, young and unaware that building relationships took intention and work. At times guilt had me shy away from actively building these relationships out of the guilt that I now know I was never expected to carry.

I now understand all I can do is be present without perfection and just love. A part of my self-care routine is forgiving myself for things I had limited control over, accepting my today and being intentional about my tomorrow

"For from his fullness we have all received, grace upon grace."[71]

What are you forgiving yourself for today? What are you allowing grace for?

<u>Day 33</u>

"Life has taught me that I am not always in control. Life is full of experience, lessons, heartbreak, and pain. But it has also shown me love, beauty, possibility, and a new beginning.

---

[71] *John 1:16 KJV*

Embrace it all. It makes us who we are, and after every storm clears the sky."

When I was younger, I remember feeling as if I had forever to accomplish my life aspirations and goals. I knew I had my youth, time...my health and with God there was nothing I could not do.

Life happened and after experiencing loss, rejection, health battles and disappointments I began to question what God's plan was for my life. I thought I had "control," I had no idea that the rug could be pulled out from under me at any given moment.

When we realize we have little control on life happenings it's important to "know" that in the midst of the storm God still is in control. Ask me how I know? A part of self-care is giving yourself permission to not carry the burden of fear, anxiety, depression, rejection, what it's of a diagnosis, or loss of a loved one by yourself. Love yourself enough to lay your burdens down...give yourself rest...carrying this alone can be so exhausting.

"Jesus Christ is the same yesterday and today and forever."
Hebrews 13:8

What are you releasing to God today?

Day 34

Be proud of how you've been handling these past months. The silent battles you fought, the moment you had to humble yourself, wiped your own tears and pat yourself on the back. Celebrate your strength.

One day you will tell your story of how you overcame what you went through and it will be someone else's survival guide.

"When the righteous cry for help, the Lord hears and delivers them out of all their troubles."[72]

What strengths will you allow yourself to celebrate?

Day 35

In my late 20's I worked at a utility company in Philadelphia for almost eight years and was blessed to meet some wonderful people I consider friends to this very day.

During my time there I developed a special bond with Ray, our gentle giant. I admired his fearlessness, courage, beautiful heart and love of travel. In his lifetime he has traveled to 67 countries! His detailed accounts of his travels will have you envisioning you were there too!

I visited Ray as he has been dealing with some health challenges. It was important for me to make sure he knew that

---

[72] *Psalms 34:17 ESV*

he mattered, he was not alone, he was not forgotten, his journey is significant and he was "seen."

Ray kept telling me that he wanted me to see the flags he had on the wall of all the countries he has traveled to in his lifetime but they had been put in storage. I repeatedly told him, those flags are "things" that represent where you've been, YOU'VE LIVED IT!!!

Whatever you do today...I hope you "live." Self-care is giving yourself "permission" to live. Ray may not be able to travel now but what beautiful memories he has to hold on to...memories to last a lifetime.

"For nothing will be impossible with God." [73]

What choices will you make and/or steps will you put in place to ensure you live during your life journey?

Day 36

You meet someone incredible but you question it. You get invited to the table but sit silently because you're too busy questioning if you belong. Good things happen in your life and you ask why. Blessings can't multiply if you are always wasting energy questioning them.

Today instead of saying why me ask yourself why not me? Self-care includes knowing you are worthy and walking in

---

[73] *Luke 1:37 ESV*

that knowledge every day. Nothing and no one can stop you from receiving what God has for you...but you can delay the process by not knowing and believing who He says you are to Him. Today, don't question your blessings but walk in them because there will be more to come.

"For all the promises of God find their Yes in him. That is why it is through him that we utter our Amen to God for his glory."[74]

Ask yourself, "Why not you?"

Day 37

My father was a man of few words but when he spoke you heard him and you listened. His words mattered and they gave me wings to fly.

I came across a picture of us that was taken the day I graduated college; I was the first in our family. The look on his face says it all, pride. I wish he was still here, I miss him every day.

The picture was a reminder for me to have that same look of pride when I see myself. I matter, legacy matters and there is still work to be done.

Today it is important to remember that even when our loved ones are no longer here that love still exists and it's in us.

---

[74] *2 Corinthians 1:20 ESV*

"He has given us the Holy Spirit to fill our hearts with His love."[75]

Are you able to see yourself the way God sees you? Have you been told you're someone other than who God confirmed in His word? What will be your affirmation of self-love today?

Day 38

A friend recently posted a picture of beautiful red roses. I remember immediately thinking, "beautiful." I began to think about the love both my parents, especially my father, had for red roses. A few years ago, I went to CVS and saw a small rose bush to plant. It was tiny but the petals were so rich and I knew mom would love it planted to remind her of my dad so I planted it that Mother's Day.

The next two years it didn't thrive. In fact, the roots had been unintentionally disturbed, bugs were eating all the leaves but we still saw life in this little rose bush. I began caring for it every day and providing it with nutrients, love and water.

The rose bush looked like something you would pull up and throw away but when it received love, gentleness, care, nutrients, focus, support with a pole I placed to help it stand up

---

[75] *Romans 5:5 NKJV*

straight and purpose to make my mom smile, it thrived. If God can do this for a plant imagine what He can do for you.

"Life itself is a privilege. But to live life to the fullest - well. That is a choice." [76]

"Do you know that you are God's temple and that God's spirit dwells in you?" [77]

If a plant needs these things to survive and thrive, why not give yourself the same? What will you implement for your self-care today?

Day 39

I remember hearing a powerful sermon on the topic of expectation. The pastor said we should get up every morning with the expectation of having a great day, being blessed...the same expectation we had as a child on Christmas morning.

A part of my self-care routine is changing my "what if not" to "God will." There was a time when I had so much doubt as to what my journey would be. There was a lady who worked at a local convenience store I frequented that would say, "good morning." She said it in a way that I knew my morning would be "good." God truly puts people in place to meet our needs. I will

---

[76] *Andy Andrews*
[77] *1 Corinthians 3:16 ESV*

never forget how she made me feel during a difficult time and the importance of expecting something great.

"God has promised that your expectation shall not be cut off because the desires of the righteous shall be great." [78] *Proverbs 10:24*

What are you expecting God for today?

Day 40

The you that's had a rough week. The you that seems to be under constant storm clouds. The you that feels invisible. The you that doesn't know how much longer you can hold on. The one that has lost faith. The you that always blames yourself for everything that goes wrong. To you. You are incredible. You make this world more wonderful. You have so much potential and so many things left to do. You have time. Better things are coming your way, so please hang in there. You can do it. - Jodi Ann Bickley

Every day is not perfect and may come with challenges outside of our control but please remember we have a God that promises that He will never leave or forsake us..."you" will never walk this journey alone.

---

[78] *Proverbs 10:24*

"Be strong and courageous. Do not be afraid or terrified because of them, for the Lord your God goes with you; He will never leave you or forsake you." [79]

...And What If You Live?

[79] *Deuteronomy 31:6 ESV*

RESOURCES

Breast Cancer Resources & Support

Financial help

Bringing Hope Home

(484) 580-8395

Bringing Hope Home gives financial and emotional support to families facing cancer. Through its Light of Hope Family Grant Program, the organization offers a one-time grant to pay essential household bills for families affected by cancer in the Greater Philadelphia Area.

Cancer*Care*

(800) 813-4673 (800-813-HOPE)

Cancer*Care* offers counseling, case management, financial assistance, support groups, educational programs, and publications for anyone living with cancer. Oncology social workers and cancer experts provide Cancer*Care* services.

Forward4Tobi

(847) 894-6650

The Forward4Tobi Foundation helps people with breast cancer and their families pay for medical, childcare, or other daily expenses. Forward4Tobi currently works with two medical centers in the United States: NorthShore University Health Systems in Evanston, IL and Dana-Farber Cancer Institute in Boston, MA.

HealthWell Foundation

(800) 675-8416

The HealthWell Foundation provides financial help with treatment-related costs, including the cost of supplies, medicine, surgeries, and travel.

PAN Foundation

(866) 316-7263 (866-316-PANF)

PAN (Patient Access Network) Foundation offers financial assistance to people who cannot afford treatment-related out-of-pocket costs. People who need assistance can complete an online application to learn more about eligibility and available funds.

The Pink Fund

(877) 234-7465 (877-234-PINK)

The Pink Fund gives short-term financial aid to people with breast cancer who are in active treatment. The Pink Fund makes direct bill payments for health insurance premiums and non-medical bill payments such as mortgage or rent, utilities, car payments, and car insurance.

Breast cancer support resources

CancerConnect

(208) 727-6880

CancerConnect provides cancer-related news, information, and peer support services to people living with cancer, caregivers, and advocates.

Cancer Support Community (CSC)
(888) 793-9355
CSC offers emotional and social support services to people living with cancer. Through its network of centers, CSC connects people to programs based on their unique needs. Services include support groups, counseling, education, and healthy lifestyle programs run by trained and licensed professionals.

FORCE: Facing Hereditary Cancer EMPOWERED
(866) 288-7475 (866-288-RISK)
FORCE provides education and support to people and families at risk for testing positive or who have tested positive for inherited gene mutations that can lead to cancer. The organization advocates for access to care and better treatment and prevention options for people facing hereditary cancer.

Imerman Angels
(866) 463-7626 (866-IMERMAN)
Imerman Angels is a support organization for people diagnosed with cancer and for caregivers of people diagnosed with cancer. Offering a free, personalized, one-on-one volunteer match with

someone who's had a similar experience, Imerman Angels connects people all over the world for phone, online, or in-person support.

LympheDIVAs
(866) 411-3482 (866-411-DIVA)

LympheDIVAs creates fashion-conscious compression apparel for people diagnosed with lymphedema, a swelling condition that can sometimes happen after breast cancer surgery.

SHARE
(844) 275-7427

SHARE connects people affected by breast, ovarian, and uterine cancers through its supportive network of others who've been diagnosed. Services include a hotline (Spanish and other languages offered), support groups, wellness programs, educational meetings, and advocacy activities.

The Tutu Project
(201) 785-7974

The Tutu Project raises funds that are distributed to nonprofit groups supporting people diagnosed with breast cancer. The organization is known for photos of its founder, and others, wearing tutus.

Young women's breast cancer resources
Rethink Breast Cancer
(416) 220-0700

Rethink Breast Cancer educates and connects young people being treated for or concerned about breast cancer. The group's advocacy work focuses on changing and improving education, research, treatment, and services.

Tigerlily Foundation
(888) 580-6253
The Tigerlily Foundation offers support for young women (ages 15-45) at high risk for or who've been diagnosed with breast cancer, including women of diverse and underserved communities. Programs focus on education, empowerment, advocacy, and support.

Young Survival Coalition (YSC)
(877) 972-1011
The Young Survival Coalition works to improve quality of life for young adults diagnosed with breast cancer and their loved ones. YSC provides breast cancer information, programs, supportive connection, and an annual summit featuring medical experts and workshops.

Male breast cancer resources

HIS Breast Cancer Awareness
HIS Breast Cancer Awareness offers education and resources to men with breast cancer and men at high risk for being diagnosed with breast cancer. By providing connection and support, the

organization works to reduce the stigma often felt by men diagnosed with breast cancer.

Male Breast Cancer Global Alliance

The MBCGA brings together men with breast cancer and researchers, clinicians, and oncologists worldwide to advance research, clinical trials, and treatments for men diagnosed with breast cancer.

Metastatic breast cancer resources

Metastatic Breast Cancer (MBC) Alliance

The Metastatic Breast Cancer Alliance works to increase awareness and education about MBC and advance policy and research through its programs.

American Brain Tumor Association (ABTA)

The American Brain Tumor Association funds brain tumor research and provides education to patients, caregivers, and loved ones. LBBC participates in ABTA's Metastatic Brain Tumor Initiative, which empowers people with metastatic brain tumors such as breast cancer brain metastasis.

MBCBrainMets.org

A website created by patient advocates living with metastatic breast cancer, this website is a one-stop resource hub for people with breast cancer brain metastasis that features cutting-edge information, community, and support.

Metastatic Breast Cancer Network (MBCN)
(888) 500-0370
The Metastatic Breast Cancer Network is an all-volunteer, patient-led advocacy organization that funds metastatic breast cancer research and provides information about diagnosis, treatment, clinical trials, research, and ways to find support.

METAvivor
METAvivor funds research on ways to extend and improve quality of life for people living with metastatic breast cancer. The organization awards grants to individuals with clinical or doctoral degrees whose research proposals show strong potential to make an impact for the stage IV community. METAvivor also raises public awareness of stage IV MBC and offers guidance for starting peer-to-peer support groups.

Theresa's Research Foundation
Theresa's Research Foundation funds research for metastatic breast cancer treatment. The foundation offers a metastatic breast cancer clinical trial search tool as well as patient-advocacy training.

Twisted Pink

(502) 890-2662

Twisted Pink raises funds and provides online connection and support for people living with metastatic breast cancer. Funding is focused on MBC treatment research and awareness.

Resources for African American women

For the Breast of Us

For the Breast of Us aims to empower women of color affected by breast cancer through education, advocacy, and community. Offerings include medical expert webinars and video roundtables with others who've been diagnosed.

The Chrysalis Initiative

(800) 929-4979

The Chrysalis Initiative offers support for Black women diagnosed with breast cancer. Chrysalis aims to make it easier for disparate groups to get care through individual coaching, mobile resources, and online learning opportunities.

Sisters Network, Inc.

(866) 781-1808

Sisters Network works to increase local and national attention to the impact breast cancer has in the Black community and shares resources for Black women affected by breast cancer.

Touch, The Black Breast Cancer Alliance

(443) 758-1924

Touch aims to improve clinical trial research and access to healthcare for Black women diagnosed with breast cancer and provides guidance for understanding and finding clinical trials. The alliance also connects Black women living with breast cancer to peers and professionals.

Resources for Jewish women

Sharsheret

(866) 474-2774

Sharsheret provides culturally sensitive education and support to young Jewish women diagnosed with breast cancer and people at risk of developing breast cancer. The organization also shares educational resources with Jewish communities and healthcare organizations.

Caregivers, family & friends

American Cancer Society Caregiver Support Video Series

Get educational support for yourself and your loved ones. Videos cover key topics like drain care, pain management, side effects, and self-care. Includes stories from caregivers of people with cancer. Check out ACS's Caregiver Resource Guide, too.

American Psychological Association Caregiver Resources

The APA offers links to self-care tips, resources to help you plan in your state or your local community, help with respite care, and more.

CancerCare Support Groups
(800) 813-4673 (800-813-HOPE)
Select from a variety of caregiver support groups online and in person, in New York and New Jersey.

CaringBridge
(651) 452-7940
CaringBridge offers free, private websites for people affected by serious illness to share health updates with friends and family. These websites also allow loved ones to send messages of support.

Conversations with Kelly Podcast
Hear from a clinical psychotherapist who maintains a healing community with the goal of minimizing suffering and honoring grief.

Family Caregiving Alliance
(800) 445-8106
FCA provides services to caregivers of adults with physical and mental difficulties, including assessment, care planning, direct

care skills, wellness programs, respite services and legal/financial consultation vouchers.

MyLifeLine.org
(888) 234-2468
MyLifeLine.org helps people with cancer and caregivers to create free personalized websites that serve as online support communities where family and friends can gather.

Government resources

Centers for Disease Control and Prevention (CDC)
(800) 232-4636 (1-800-CDC-INFO)
The CDC is a national public health agency that shares guidance and information about many health conditions, including breast cancer. CDC has up-to-date information on breast cancer risk factors, symptoms, statistics, research, and treatments. The agency also helps people access mammograms and screening programs through its National Breast and Cervical Cancer Early Detection Program (NBCCEDP).

National Breast and Cervical Cancer Early Detection Program (CDC)
(800) 232-4636
A program of the CDC, NBCCEDP provides access to screenings and services for women with low income and women who are uninsured or underserved.

National Cancer Institute (NCI)

(800) 422-6237

NCI is a resource for learning about all types of cancer, including breast cancer. NCI also shares information about ongoing research in breast cancer.

Project Facilitate (FDA)

(301) 796 3400

Project Facilitate helps oncology specialists and people living with cancer learn about and access clinical trials.

U.S. Food and Drug Administration (FDA)

(888) 463-6332 (1-888-INFO-FDA)

The FDA offers the most up-to-date information about approved cancer medicines, including treatment safety, side effects, label changes, and recall news.

National Institute of Health's National Library of Medicine (NLM)

NLM hosts MedLine Plus, which offers information on topics such as health and wellness, medicines, and genetics. NLM also has a tool to help people find clinical trials and learn about new treatments.

Education and research resources

American Association for Cancer Research (AACR)

(215) 440-9300

AACR programs support cancer researchers and offer resources for people affected by cancer, including education, personal stories, and Cancer Today magazine.

American Cancer Society (ACS)
(800) 227-2345
ACS maintains a website with information about all types of cancer, including news, research, statistics, and tips for living with cancer. Breast cancer topics cover risk, early detection, and understanding diagnosis, treatment, and reconstruction.

Breastcancer.org
(610) 642-6550
Breastcancer.org provides information about breast cancer, including tests, types of breast cancer, treatment options, and clinical trial news. Breastcancer.org also features expert podcasts and personal stories from people who've been diagnosed.

BreastCancerTrials.org (BCT)
(888) 282-7099
BreastCancerTrials.org encourages people living with breast cancer to consider clinical trials as a normal part of care. The organization educates people about trials and offers tools to make it easier to find trials specific to a person's breast cancer diagnosis and treatment history.

Cancer.Net by American Society of Clinical Oncology (ASCO)
(571) 483-1780
Cancer.Net is an educational resource for people diagnosed with cancer and their caregivers. The site offers information about many kinds of cancer including breast cancer. Cancer.Net also offers publications, expert health blogs, and monthly e-newsletters.

Cure Today
(609) 716-7777
Cure Today is a magazine and online resource presenting cancer research news coverage, patient stories, and more. Living Beyond Breast Cancer is proud to partner with Cure Today to offer the latest medical news and empowering stories to people affected by breast cancer.

Inflammatory Breast Cancer (IBC) Research Foundation
(877) 786-7422 (877-STOP-IBC)
IBC Research Foundation offers information, education, and advocacy for people diagnosed with inflammatory breast cancer. The foundation supports and summarizes research on the causes of IBC and IBC treatment research.

Lobular Breast Cancer Alliance (LBCA)
LBCA is a network of patient advocates diagnosed with lobular breast cancer and working with breast cancer researchers and

clinicians. The alliance strives to increase knowledge of lobular breast disease and promote research that leads to advances in prevention, diagnosis, treatment, and follow-up care.

National Accreditation Program for Breast Centers (NAPBC)
NAPBC is run by the American College of Surgeons and offers accreditation to centers that provide breast cancer care. Breast centers accredited through NAPBC must comply with standards of care, which aim to offer timely, modern, high-quality care based on scientific research. NAPBC's search tool helps people find accredited breast centers.

National Coalition for Cancer Survivorship (NCCS)
NCCS advocates for improved research, regulation, funding, and delivery of cancer care. Through its programs and resources, the group provides tools for self-advocacy to people who've been treated for cancer. NCCS also helps other organizations address public policy issues that affect people living with cancer.

National Lymphedema Network (NLN)
NLN offers education and guidance for understanding and managing lymphedema, a swelling condition that can sometimes happen after breast cancer surgery.

Not Putting on a Shirt
(412) 407-5997

Not Putting on a Shirt shares information and support for people who choose to not undergo breast reconstruction after mastectomy.

OncoLink
(215) 349-8895
OncoLink, managed by the University of Pennsylvania, provides a complete database of information about specific types of cancer, updates on cancer treatments, and news about research advances.

Research Advocacy Network (RAN)
(877) 276-2187
RAN works to improve patient-focused cancer research through collaboration with other cancer-centered groups, scientists, and advocates.

Susan G. Komen
(877) 465-6636 (877-GO-KOMEN)
Susan G. Komen works to fund and improve breast cancer research, community health, global outreach, and public policy initiatives. Offerings include information about breast cancer, clinical trials, and advocacy.

Triple Negative Breast Cancer Foundation
Helpline: (877) 880-8622 (877-880-TNBC)

Main office: (646) 942-0242

This organization provides information on triple-negative breast cancer and funds research on treatment. The foundation also offers an online community, webinars, downloadable guides, and financial help.

You can also explore LBBC educational resources on diagnosis, treatment, side effects, emotional health, and more in our About breast cancer section.

Transportation resources

Angel Flight East (AFE)

(215) 358-1900

Angel Flight East gives free air transportation to children and adults who need medical treatments far from home. AFE's volunteers serve the Northeastern United States and link with other volunteer pilot organizations for stops beyond its reach.

Coaching Services

Ray Janeen Stevens

Certified Life Coach and Founder of ...And What If You Live?
(856) 267-3853

Committed to assisting those looking to move forward from a diagnosis, discover new direction, create new purpose, and live more aligned with their values.

Legal services

Cancer Legal Resource Center (CLRC)

(866) 843-2572 (866-THE-CLRC)

CLRC provides information and supportive resources for cancer-related legal, job, and insurance issues.

Triage Cancer

(424) 258-4628

Triage Cancer educates people diagnosed with cancer and caregivers about legal and practical issues. The organization offers information, events, and downloadable guides on topics such as managing health insurance, finances, and employment after a diagnosis.

Other resources

A Fresh Chapter

A Fresh Chapter provides educational and leadership workshops, volunteer programs, and support for people impacted by cancer. Through virtual and on-site programs around the world, AFC works to help people emotionally recover from experiences with cancer.

American Cancer Society's Look Good Feel Better Program

(800) 227-2345

Look Good Feel Better works to improve self-image, confidence, and quality of life for people undergoing cancer treatment. The program offers free group workshops, salon consultations, and guidance on skin and nail care, makeup, head coverings, and wigs.

Anticancer Lifestyle Program (ACLP)
(603) 226-4408
ACLP is an online lifestyle course for people diagnosed with cancer and people who want to reduce their risk of many conditions including cancer.

Breast Advocate App for iPhone and Android
This free app, designed for people diagnosed with breast cancer or at risk of developing breast cancer, provides personalized information about breast cancer surgery and reconstruction options, as well as access to research news.

Healwell
(703) 662-1603
Healwell offers massage therapy designed for people diagnosed with cancer or other serious illnesses, as well as caregivers. Serving the Washington, DC metro area, Healwell has inpatient and outpatient services. Healwell also trains massage therapists on how to adapt massage techniques to the unique needs of people with serious illness.

My Hope Chest
(727) 642-4243

My Hope Chest educates people diagnosed with breast cancer about breast reconstruction surgery. The organization also funds uninsured and underinsured women who cannot afford reconstruction surgery.

Mary's Place by the Sea
(732)-455-5344
Mary's Place by the Sea gives any woman facing cancer a place to pause from their daily challenges in a supportive and relaxing environment.

(Some resources courtesy of Living Beyond Breast Cancer)

ABOUT THE AUTHOR

Ray Janeen Stevens, M.S. is a breast cancer survivor, certified life coach, author, speaker and founder of *"...And What If You Live?"* She is a graduate of Eastern University with a Master's degree in Nonprofit Management and has worked in leadership as a Development Director for various nonprofit organizations for over 20 years.

Her purpose is to support and inspire those experiencing a cancer diagnosis, life obstacles, or in a caregiving role to live with greater self-awareness, new perspective and self-empowerment through life coaching.

In addition, *"...And What If You Live"* was established as a 501(C) 3 nonprofit organization as a way to give back to the community. It is the mission of *"...And What If You Live"* to assist those seeking to move forward from a diagnosis and life change to discover new direction, create new purpose, and live more aligned with their values.

Ray Janeen is a proud mother to one daughter Jameka Fisher, gigi Ray to Maliya Clark, godmother to Nayomi Angueiro and auntie to a host of nieces and nephews.

Made in the USA
Middletown, DE
16 February 2023

24912961R00097